Two-Dimensional CAD
City & Guilds 4351-01
Level 3
for
AutoCAD 2000

COMPLETED EXAMINATION PAPERS

J.T. Roberts, B.Sc., M.Sc.

Published by

Payne-Gallway Publishers Ltd

76 -78 Christchurch Street

Ipswich IP4 2DE

Tel: 01473 251097

Fax: 01473 232758

E-mail payne_gallway@compuserve.com

2000

Acknowledgements

I would like to thank Pat and Oliver Heathcote at Payne-Gallway for their enthusiasm and advice.

First edition 2000

A catalogue entry for this book is available from the British Library
ISBN 1 903112 24 9

All trademarks are recognised

Printed in Great Britain by
WM Print Ltd, Walsall, West Midlands, England.

To
Monica

Contents

Preface
Conventions used in this Book

Text in a **Bold** style signifies an AutoCAD command or dialogue box text to be either accessed through the keyboard, screen icons or pull-down menus e.g. **DRAW/Line**. Icons used at the side of the page indicate that the command and/or selection can be accessed through that button.

Paragraph numbers, 3.3, 3.4 etc, are cross-referenced to the C&G syllabus - see note below.

References are made to turning Snap, Grid and Ortho to On etc. Toggling their use is generally left to the discretion of the user.

This book is intended to be used in the study of the examinations:-

The *City & Guilds Certificate in Two-Dimensional Computer-Aided Design Level 3, Course No. 4351-01* from September 1999. The assignment syllabus must be used in conjunction with this book.

All pre-prepared drawings, files and completed assignments can be downloaded from the publisher's website at **www.payne-gallway.co.uk**.

The intended audience

It is assumed that the student has undertaken an introductory course on AutoCAD prior to embarking on this course of study. A book entitled *Introduction to AutoCAD 2000* by JT Roberts, can be used as an introduction to this course and is available from the publisher. Please see ordering details at the end of this book.

The methods described in this book are not meant to be prescriptive and definitive. They are the way in which I approached the problems. I have not necessarily used the latest AutoCAD 2000 commands but have tried to use the commands which will give a solid grounding and understanding, bearing in mind the level of the audience. You will, however, see the AutoCAD 2000 icons at the page side. I have tried to vary the input mechanisms - using a pull-down menu, the command line and the command icons but as you progress you will develop your own preferences.

Any improvements, corrections, omissions and/or constructive criticism would be gratefully accepted.

Please contact me at my e-mail address:- **jeffroberts@72fernlea.freeserve.co.uk**

Jeff Roberts

Introduction

Candidate Eligibility

The selection of candidates is at the discretion of the assessment centre. Previous knowledge is not necessary although it is advantageous to have undertaken an introductory CAD course. Familiarity with basic geometric concepts and coordinate geometry would also be helpful.

Examination Papers

The assessments comprise 4 multi-choice question papers (MCQ), and 9 practical assignments. The assessment programme requires you to attempt 1 paper from the **Multiple Choice Questions**, 1 from the section on **Creating Drawings**, 1 from **Editing, Dimensioning and Use of Blocks**, and the single mandatory paper **Creating a Template**.

The intention is that you practise the practical assignments until you feel proficient enough to attempt one of the papers which is chosen at random by yourself or your tutor. This only applies where there are multiple choices, of course.

Practical Assignment PA 4351-01-TDPA - Creating a Template

This is the only assignment where a choice is not given. It must be completed as the first practical assessment as this completed template drawing is needed for insertion into the assessment papers PA 4351-01 to 04 that follow.

The assignment is to draw a border which includes 4 named layers, 2 text styles, a suitable point entity setting, and the insertion of a pre-prepared image file of a suitable logo. Model Space and Paper Space limits must be set correctly and a folder (directory) created with the drawing template file saved in this folder. You are allowed 30 minutes for this assignment.

Practical Assignment - PA 4351-01 to 04 - Creating Drawings

The requirement of this assignment is to use the practical assignment **PA 4351-01-TDPA** prepared by yourself and to create a range of objects within the border in the time limit of 2.5 hours.

The border drawn in the previous assignment is opened in Paper Space and drawing title and personal border information etc. are created.

In Model Space objects are created which include isometrics, hatching, broken lines, solid-fills, an inserted pre-prepared text file and the creation of an additional viewport.

The drawing must be saved onto a floppy disk and a hard copy produced at a scale of 1:1.

Practical Assignment - PA 4351-05 to 08 - Editing, Dimensioning and Use of Blocks

The assignment is divided into 2 parts. The objective of Part 1 is to edit a pre-produced drawing. Part 2 also uses a pre-produced drawing for you to dimension. In addition, Part 2 requires you to produce a drawing utilising blocks and associated attribute data. The assignment is of 2.5 hours duration and the drawing must be saved onto a floppy disk but a hard copy is not required.

Multiple Choice Question Test

The MCQ tests comprise 4 assessments each containing 14 questions. You must answer 10 questions correctly in 30 minutes to pass. You will gain the knowledge to answer these questions successfully through the practical tests and by studying the AutoCAD manual. It follows, therefore, that the MCQ tests would usually be taken on completion of the practical assignments although there is no hard and fast rule on this.

Resitting an Assignment

If you fail any of the assignments 7 days must elapse before a resit can be attempted. The failed assignment must be taken out of the random choice so the choice of resit assignments is reduced to 3. This does not apply to the **4351-01-TDPA** assignment which will be attempted again after 7 days have elapsed.

Alternative Assessment

You may submit alternative material which has been produced by yourself and must be of an equivalent competence level. However, at least 1 of the practical assignments provided must be undertaken.

Marking Scheme

The marking scheme for the practical assignments is that all objectives marked with a [] must be achieved successfully. Failure to meet an objective marked with a () is regarded as a minor error. Practical assignment **4351-01-TDPA** allows 2 minor errors, **4351-01-01** to **04** allow 2 minor errors and **4351-01-05** to **08** allow 1 minor error.

Log Book

The Log Book is required to be completed by the candidate as each competence is achieved and should be signed and dated. The tutor will check the Log Book and it will also be verified for completion by the external City & Guilds examiner.
Objective references marked with a '(P)' indicate that the competence is measured through the practical assessments. Objective references marked with a '(W)' indicate that the competence is measured through the written assessments.

Errors in the City & Guilds documentation

There are some errors and omissions in the documentation and where these occur they are described in the relevant section and alternative suggestions are made. You must, however, agree to alternative actions with your tutor.

PA 4351-01-TDPA

Target Drawing

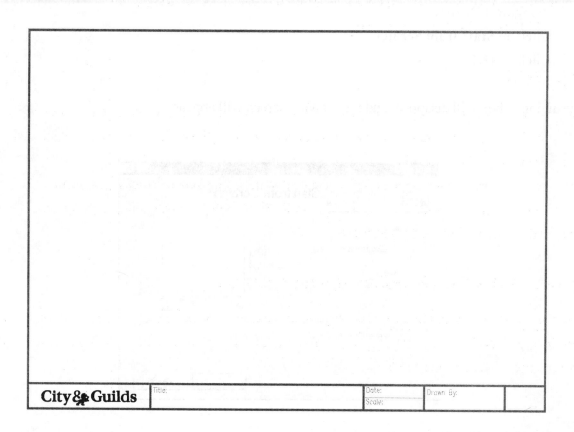

City&Guilds	Title:		Date:	Drawn By:	
			Scale:		

Pre-prepared files

To complete this assignment a pre-prepared image file is needed. Your tutor will provide you with the pre-prepared **'C&Glogo.wmf'** file or similar. You may also download the file from the publisher's website at www.payne-gallway.co.uk.

3.2

Creating a new Drawing Template

■ Execute the AutoCAD software and the **Start Up** dialogue box will appear as shown in Figure TDPA-1.

■ Click on **Start from Scratch**.

■ Click on **OK**.

The dialogue box will disappear and the drawing screen will appear.

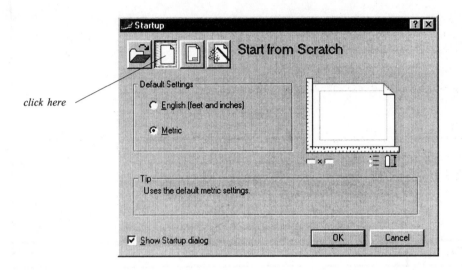

Figure TDPA-1. The Start Up Dialogue box

3.3
Setting Model-Space Limits

We are required to resize the drawing 'sheet' and for this we will use **FORMAT/Drawing Limits**. As your initial limits may not be set to the default we need to **VIEW/Zoom/All** after the **Limits** command because AutoCAD does not automatically change the screen view after drawing limits have been changed.

■ At the command line type **Limits**.

Command: **'_limits**
Reset Model space limits:
Specify lower left corner or [ON/OFF] <0.0000,0.0000>:   **Enter**
Specify upper right corner <420.0000,297.0000>:   **Enter**

■ From the pull-down use **VIEW/Zoom/All**

Command: **zoom**
Specify corner of window, enter a scale factor (nX or nXP), or [All/Center/Dynamic/Extents/Previous/Scale/Window] <real time>:   **a (for all)**
Regenerating model.

3.4
Creating New Layers

We are required to create 4 new layers with different colours and **Continuous** and **Centre**
linestyles.
Before creating the layers we need to load the **Center** (American spelling) linetype as
AutoCAD only automatically loads the **Continuous** linetype.

■ Use **FORMAT/Layer** and the **Layer Properties Manager** dialogue box will appear as
shown in Figure TDPA-2.

At this stage it shows only the **Continuous** linetype loaded.

■ Click on **Continuous** and the **Select Linetype** dialogue box will appear.
■ Click on **Load** and the **Load or Reload Linetypes** dialogue box will appear as shown in
Figure TDPA-2.
■ Scroll down and click on **Center**.
■ Click on **OK**.

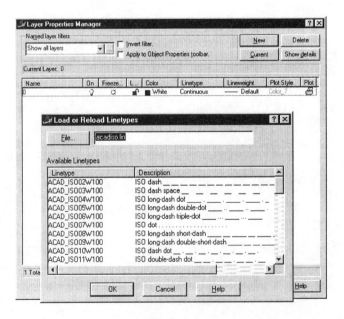

Figure TDPA-2. *Layer Properties Manager dialogue box with Load or Reload Linetypes
dialogue box overlaying it.*

The **Center** linetype is added to the list in the **Select Linetype** dialogue box.

- Click on **OK**.
- Activate the **Layer Properties Manager** dialogue box by clicking on the **Layers** button.
- Click on **New** and the word **Layer1** will appear in the list as shown in Figure TDPA-3.
- Overtype this with **Hatch.**
- Click on **New** each time, add the 3 remaining layer names and change the linetype as required.

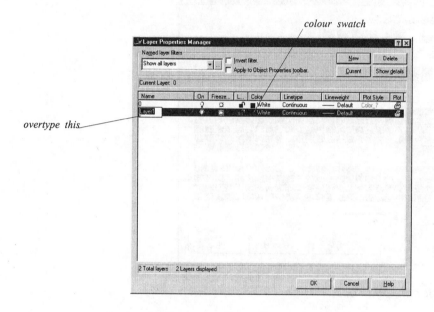

Figure TDPA-3. *Layer Properties Manager dialogue box*

To Change the 'Hatch' Layer Colour

- Click on the colour swatch as shown in Figure TDPA-3.
- The **Select Color** dialogue box will appear overlaying the **Layers Properties Manager** dialogue box as shown in Figure TDPA-4.
- Click on **Green** in the **Standard Colors** box as shown in Figure TDPA-4.
- Click on **OK**.

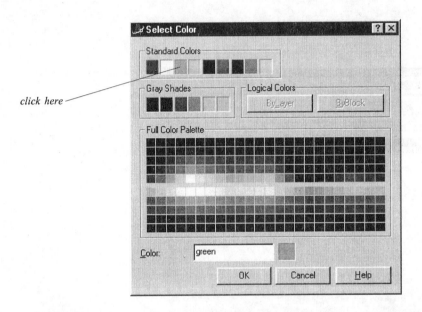

Figure TDPA-4. Select Color dialogue box

The **Select Color** dialogue box will disappear, the **Layer Properties Manager** dialogue box will reappear and you will see that the layer **Hatch** has now been assigned the colour **Green**.

■   Repeat for the other 3 layers assigning the colours as required.

To change the linetype for the Centre Layer

■   Click on the word **Continuous** on the **Centre** layer in the **Layers Properties Manager** dialogue box and the **Select Linetype** dialogue box will appear as shown in Figure TDPA-5.

■   Click on the **Center** style.

■   Click on **OK**.

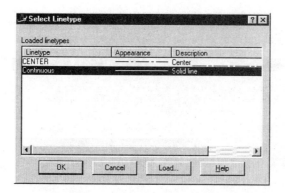

Figure TDPA-5. *Select Linetype dialogue box*

The **Select Linetype** dialogue box will disappear and the **Center** layer has now been assigned the **Center** linetype in the Layer Properties Manager dialogue box.

■   Click on **OK**.

To set Psvports as the Current layer

■   Select the layer name, **PSVports**.

■   Click on **Current**.

■   Click on **OK**.

3.5
Creating New Text Styles

■   To create the new text styles use **FORMAT/Text Style**.

The **Text Styles** dialogue box will appear as shown in Figure TDPA-6.

■   Click on **New** and the **New Text Style** dialogue box will overlay the previous.
■   Type in **CGMAIN** as a new style.
■   Click on **OK**.

The new style name automatically appears in the **Style Name** box of the **Text Style** dialogue box.

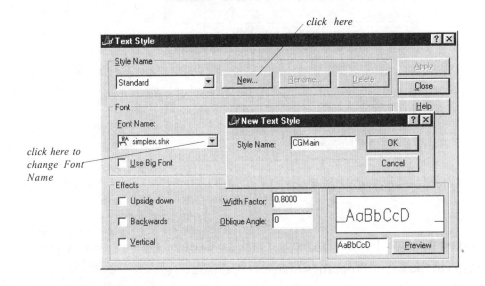

Figure TDPA-6. Text Style dialogue box

To change **CGMAIN** to a **Simplex** font
■   Click on the **Font Name** slider bar, scroll and click on **simplex.shx** as shown in Figure TDPA-6.
■   In the **Width Factor** box type **0.8** as the width of the text.
■   Click on **Apply**.
■   Repeat the process to create **CGITALIC**, using **italic.shx** with a width factor of **1.0**.
■   Click on **Apply** and **Close**.

3.6

Setting the Point Style

- From the pull-down menu change the point mode with **FORMAT/Point Style** and the **Point Style** dialogue box will appear as shown in Figure TDPA-7.
- Click on the point style as shown in Figure TDPA-7.
- Click on **OK**.

The **Point** command will now generate a cross on the drawing.

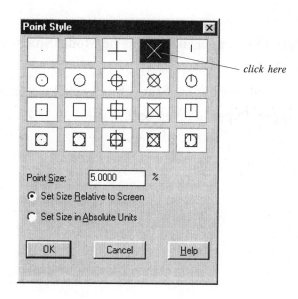

Figure TDPA-7. *Point Style dialogue box*

3.7
Setting Paper Space Limits

To set the Paper Space Limits

■   Click on the **Layout1** tab and the drawing editor changes to **Paper Space**.

The **Page Setup** dialogue box appears in which you can specify layout size and plotter settings.

■   Configure your plotter and the layout size if they are not already done.

■   Click on **OK**.

The **UCS** (User Coordinate System) changes from the **Model Space** icon to the **Paper Space** icon as shown in Figure TDPA-8.

MODEL

PAPER

A short cut is available through the bottom **Status bar** by clicking on **Model** to change to **Paper Space** and clicking on **Paper** to revert back.

To set the **Paper Space** drawing limits

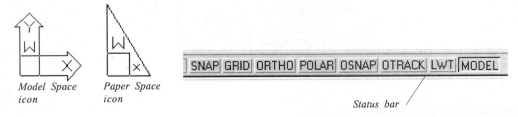

Model Space icon   Paper Space icon

Status bar

Figure TDPA-8. *Model Space icon, Paper Space icon and the Status bar*

MODEL

■   Click on **Model** to set to **Paper Space** first.

■   Use **TOOLS/Options** and the **Options** dialogue box will appear.

■   Click on the **Display** tab.

■   Click off **Display Margins** and **Display Paper background**.

Unless you do this AutoCAD will not allow paper space margins to be set.

■ Use **FORMAT/Drawing Limits** and the command line will read

Command:	*limits*
Reset Paper space limits:	
ON/OFF/<Lower left corner> <0.00,0.00>:	*Return*
Upper right corner <19000.00,12850.00>:	*265, 190*
Command:	*zoom*
All/Center/Dynamic/Extents/Left/Previous/Vmax/Window/<Scale(X/XP)>:	*all*
Regenerating drawing.	

 We need to **VIEW/Zoom/All** again after the **Limits** command because AutoCAD does not automatically change the screen view after drawing limits have been changed.

To create a **Paper Space** viewport

■ From the pull-down menu use **VIEW/Viewports/1 Viewport** and the command line will read

Command:	*_-vports*
Specify corner of viewport or	
[ON/OFF/Fit/Hideplot/Lock/Object/Polygonal/Restore/2/3/4] <Fit>:	*0, 0*
Specify opposite corner:	*265, 190*
Regenerating model.	

3.8

Drawing the Border

■ Make the layer **Title** the **Current** layer.

The border has a line width of 1 so we have to use the **Polyline** command to set that line width.

Command:	***pline***
From point:	***5, 5***
Current line-width is 0.00	
Arc/Close/Halfwidth/Length/Undo/Width/<Endpoint of line>:	***w***
Starting width <0.00>:	***1***
Ending width <1.00>:	***Enter***
Arc/Close/Halfwidth/Length/Undo/Width/<Endpoint of line>:	***5, 185***
Arc/Close/Halfwidth/Length/Undo/Width/<Endpoint of line>:	***260, 185***
Arc/Close/Halfwidth/Length/Undo/Width/<Endpoint of line>:	***260, 5***
Arc/Close/Halfwidth/Length/Undo/Width/<Endpoint of line>:	***C***

To draw the border vertical lines detail we can use the polyline command again

Command:	***pline***
From point:	***60, 5***
Current line-width is 1.00	
Arc/Close/Halfwidth/Length/Undo/Width/<Endpoint of line>:	***60, 17***
Arc/Close/Halfwidth/Length/Undo/Width/<Endpoint of line>:	***Enter***

Command:	***pline***
From point:	***170, 5***
Current line-width is 1.00	
Arc/Close/Halfwidth/Length/Undo/Width/<Endpoint of line>:	***170, 17***
Arc/Close/Halfwidth/Length/Undo/Width/<Endpoint of line>:	***Enter***

Command:	***pline***
From point:	***200, 5***
Current line-width is 1.00	
Arc/Close/Halfwidth/Length/Undo/Width/<Endpoint of line>:	***200, 17***
Arc/Close/Halfwidth/Length/Undo/Width/<Endpoint of line>:	***Enter***

Command:	***pline***
From point:	***240, 5***
Current line-width is 1.00	
Arc/Close/Halfwidth/Length/Undo/Width/<Endpoint of line>:	***240, 17***
Arc/Close/Halfwidth/Length/Undo/Width/<Endpoint of line>:	***Enter***

Command:	***pline***
From point:	***5, 17***
Current line-width is 1.00	
Arc/Close/Halfwidth/Length/Undo/Width/<Endpoint of line>:	***260, 17***
Arc/Close/Halfwidth/Length/Undo/Width/<Endpoint of line>:	***Enter***

■ Draw a line from the **Midpoints** of the vertical lines as shown in Figure TDPA-9.

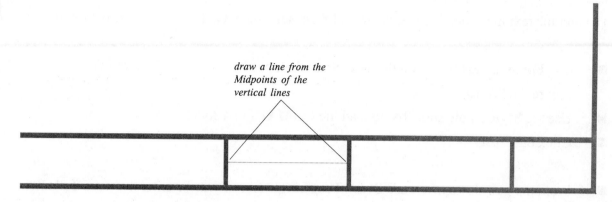

draw a line from the
Midpoints of the
vertical lines

Figure TDPA-9. *The border showing the position of the horizontal line*

Entering the Text on the Layer Title

■ With the **Format/Layer** command ensure that the layer **Title** is current and the **Layer Properties Manager** dialogue box will appear.

■ Click on **Title**.

■ Click on **Current**.

■ Click on **OK**.

■ Use **VIEW/Zoom/Window** to enlarge the bottom border.

To enter the text in the detail boxes we must first ensure that **CGMAIN** text style is loaded.

■ Use **Format/Text Style** and the **Text Style** dialogue box will appear as shown in Figure TDPA-10.

■ Use the **Style Name** slider bar to load the **CGMAIN** text style.

■ Click on **Close**.

■ From the pull-down menu use **Draw/Text/Single Line Text**. To enter the word **Title:**

Command:	*_dtext*
Current text style: "CGMAIN" Text height: 2.5000	
Specify start point of text or [Justify/Style]:	***pick** the start point of the T for 'Title:'*
Specify height <2.5000>:	***Enter***
Specify rotation angle of text <0>:	***Enter***
Enter text:	***Title:*** *Enter*
Enter text:	***Enter***

■ Repeat the **Draw/Text/Single Line Text** command for the **Date:**, **Scale:** and **Drawn by:** entries.

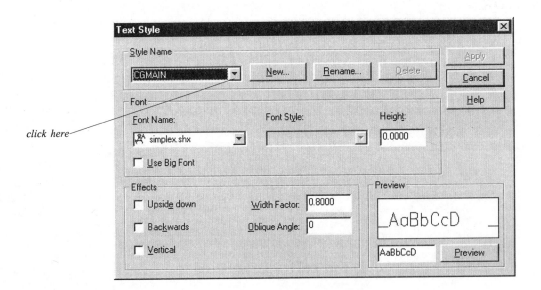

Figure TDPA-10. *Text Style dialogue box with CGMAIN as the text style*

3.9

Importing an Image File

The pre-prepared C&G logo image is in the Windows-Metafile Format.

- From the pull-down menu use the **Insert/Windows Metafile** command and the **Import WMF** dialogue box will appear as shown in Figure TDPA-11.

The image will either be on a floppy disk supplied to you by your tutor or will be in a folder/directory which your tutor will indicate to you.

- Click on the name of the image file.
- Click on **Open**.
- Drag the image file to its position as required. Use the handles to resize the image to fit the detail box.

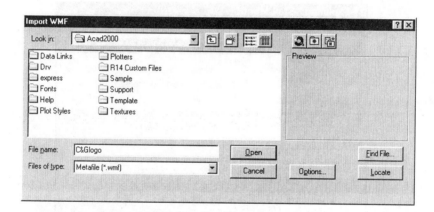

Figure TDPA-11*. Import WMF dialogue box*

3.10

Creating a New Folder/Directory

To create a new folder called **CGTEMPS**

- Place the cursor over the **START** button (Windows 95/NT) and **right** click on the mouse.
- Left click on **Explore**.

The **Exploring-Start Menu** screen will appear with a split screen showing folders and folder contents as shown in Figure TDPA-12. This will vary according to how the system is set up. Your tutor will indicate where the new folder **CGTEMPS** is to be located.

- Use **File/New** and a second pull-down menu will appear.
- Click on **Folder** and a folder icon will appear with the words **New Folder** next to it.
- Type **CGTEMPS** and the new folder will adopt this name as shown in TDPA-11.

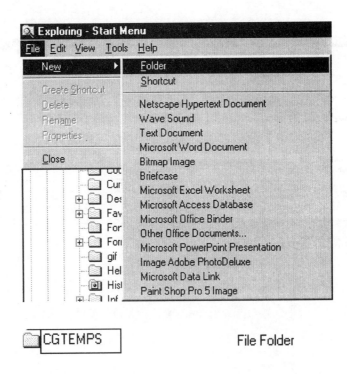

Figure TDPA-12.Exploring-Start Menu dialogue box and folder name detail.

To Save the Template Drawing

- Click on **File/Save** and the **Save Drawing As** dialogue box will appear as shown in Figure TDPA-13.
- Enter the filename **CG-TDPA** and at the **Save as type** select **Drawing Template File**.
- Click on the **Save in** window.
- Click on the folder **CGTEMPS**.
- Click on **Save**.

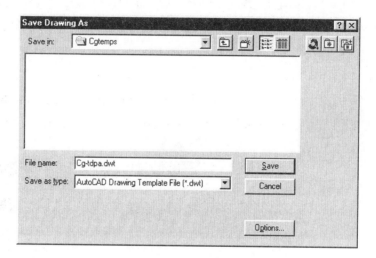

Figure TDPA-13. Save Drawing As dialogue box.

3.12

Saving the Template Drawing to a Floppy Disk

- To save the completed exercise to floppy disk use **FILE/Save As** and the **Save Drawing As** dialogue box will appear as shown in Figure TDPA-13.
- Click on the **Save in** scroll window and click on **3½ floppy drive [A]** and the file will be saved to the floppy disk. In the examination you must hand this to your tutor.

PA1 4351-01-01

Target Drawing

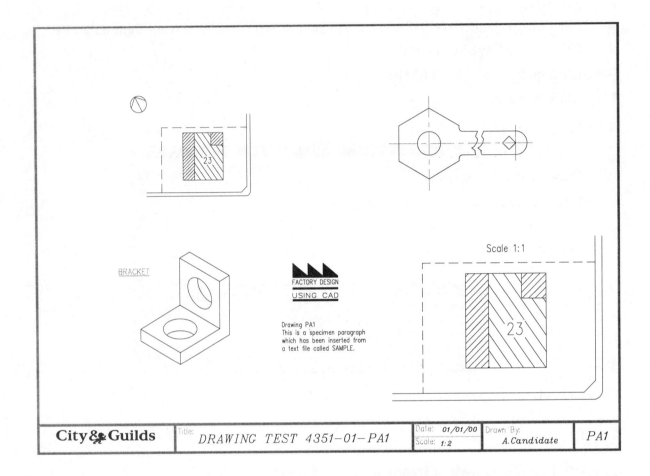

City & Guilds	Title: DRAWING TEST 4351-01-PA1	Date: 01/01/00	Drawn By:	PA1
		Scale: 1:2	A.Candidate	

Pre-prepared files

To complete this assignment a pre-prepared text file is needed. Your tutor will provide you with the pre-prepared **'PA01.TXT'** file. You may also download the file from the publisher's website at www.payne-gallway.co.uk.

3.2

Creating a new Drawing with Template Drawing CG-TDPA

- Execute the AutoCAD software and the **Start Up** dialogue box will appear.
- Click on **Use a Template** as shown in Figure 1.1.
- Click on **Browse**.

The **Select a Template file** dialogue box will appear.

- Search for the location of the folder **CGTEMPS** which contains the template file **CG-TDPA.dwt**.
- Click on this filename.
- Click on **Open** to open the template drawing.

As the template drawing was saved in **Paper Space** mode, it should still open in that mode.

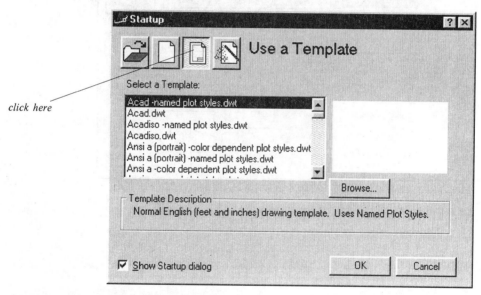

click here

Figure 1.1. The Start Up dialogue box

3.3

Setting the Current Layer to 0

- To set layer **0** as the current layer, in the **Layer Properties Manager** dialogue box click on the layer name **0**.
- Click on **Current**.
- Click on **OK**.

3.4

Completing the Title Bar

To complete the title bar text we must use the **CGITALIC** text style.

To set CGITALIC as the Current Text Style

- Use **FORMAT/Text Style** and the **Text Style** dialogue box will appear as shown in Figure 1.2.

- Click on the **Style Name** pull-down and click on the name **CGITALIC**. The Font Name **Italic.shx** and a width factor of **1** should be loaded.

- Click on **Close** to close the dialogue box.

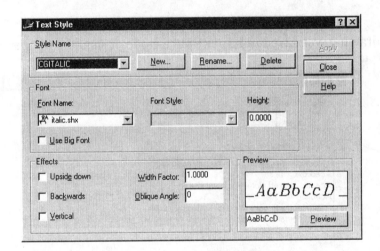

***Figure 1.2**. The Text style dialogue box*

Entering the Drawing Number

Before entering the text it will be advisable to enlarge the title bar with the **VIEW/Zoom/Window** command.

We will enter the title and the drawing number first with a text height of 3.5. The drawing number must be in the middle of the box. To ensure this we can draw a temporary line across the middle of the box from the **Midpoint** of line 1, **Perpendicular** to line 2 and then place the text **PA1** as shown in Figure 1.3.

To place the text we will use the **middle** alignment option using the **Midpoint** of the temporary line to place the text exactly in the middle of the box.

■ Use the **DRAW/Line** command to draw the temporary line

Command: _line Specify next point:	***_mid of** (pick the Midpoint of line 1)*
Specify next point:	***_per to** (pick Perpendicular to line 2)*
Specify next point:	***Enter***

Use **DRAW/Text/Single Line Text** to enter the words **PA1**

Command:	***_dtext***
Current text style: "CGITALIC" Text height: 0.2000	
Specify start point of text or [Justify/Style] :	***m** (for middle alignment)*
Specify middle point of text:	***_mid of** (pick the midpoint of the temporary line)*
Specify height <0.2000>:	***3.5***
Specify rotation angle of text <0>:	***Enter***
Enter text:	***PA1** **Enter***
Enter text:	***Enter***

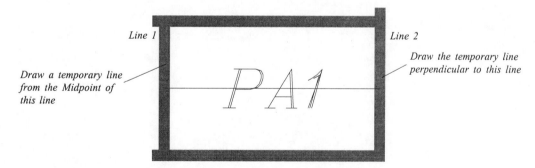

Line 1

Line 2

Draw the temporary line perpendicular to this line

Draw a temporary line from the Midpoint of this line

Figure 1.3. *The drawing number box showing the construction line before being erased*

■ **MODIFY/Erase** the temporary line.

■ To enter the title, repeat the above **DRAW/Text/Single Line Text** command but pick a start point as shown in Figure 1.4.

Command: _dtext_
Current text style: "CGITALIC" Text height: 3.500
Specify start point of text or [Justify/Style]: ***pick*** *a start point for the letter 'D' of Drawing*
Height <3.5000>: ***Enter***
Rotation angle <0>: ***Enter***
Text: ***DRAWING TEST 4351-01-PA1*** *(Enter)*
Text: ***Enter***

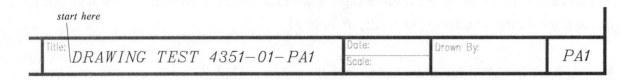

start here

Title:		Date:	Drawn By:	
DRAWING TEST 4351–01–PA1		Scale:		PA1

Figure 1.4 *The partly finished PA1 title block*

■ Repeat the **DRAW/Text/Single Line Text** command to complete the **Date, Scale** and **Drawn By** details but with text heights of **2** and **2.5** respectively.

■ **Zoom/All** when completed.

3.5

Drawing the Building Plan

PAPER ■ Change the drawing mode to **Model Space** by clicking on the **Paper** button.

3.6

Using an Appropriate Linetype

To start drawing the building load and set to the broken linetype.

■ From the **Format** pull-down menu pick **Linetype** and the **Linetype Manager** dialogue box will appear as shown in Figure 1.5.

■ Click on **Load** and load the **Dashed** linestyle.

■ Click on **Show Details** to alter the **Current Object Scale** to about **3**.

■ Click on **OK**.

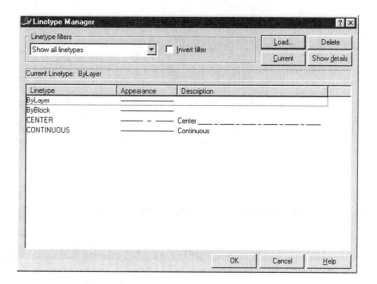

Figure 1.5 *Linetype Manager dialogue box*

Drawing the Dashed Linestyle

■ Click on the **Dashed** linetype and **Current** in the **Linetype Manager** dialogue box to make the **Dashed** linetype **Current**.

 ■ **Draw** the **Dashed** linestyle starting at the specified coordinates of **65, 190**.

Drawing the Boundary Line

- In the **Linetype Manager** dialogue box click on **Bylayer** and **Current** to make the linetype associated with its layer **Current**.
- **Draw** the boundary line starting at coordinates **51.60, 190** as shown in Figure 1.6.
- Finish above the top right of the broken line to the correct distance.

- **MODIFY/Offset** these **2** lines by **3** units outwards.
- **MODIFY/Fillet** the new line with a radius of **4** as shown in Figure 1.6.
- **MODIFY/Chamfer** the inner line with **first** and **second** distances of **5** as shown in Figure 1.6.

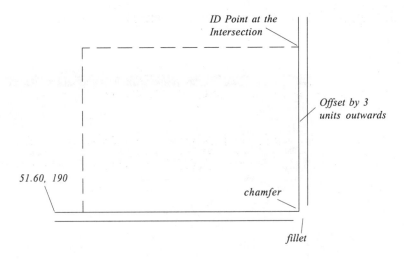

Figure 1.6 The boundary lines about to be Offset and Chamfered

Drawing the Building Outline

To draw the building outline we need to place it in the exact position within the boundary. To do this we can use the **INQUIRY/ID Point** command which will identify a coordinate location with x,y,z coordinate values. Using relative coordinates with the next command (**DRAW/Line** in our case) locates points relative to that **ID** point and we can complete the outline of the building. The **ID** point is shown in Figure 1.6.

Command: '_id Specify point:	*_int of*
	(pick the intersection as shown in Figure 1.6) X = 140.0000 Y = 245.0000 Z = 0.0000
Command: _line Specify first point:	*@-56.4, -4.5 (locates the top left of the building relative to the ID point)*
Specify next point or [Undo]:	*@40<270 (second point as shown in Figure 1.7)*
Specify next point or [Undo]:	*@35<0*
Specify next point or [Close/Undo]:	*@40<90*
Specify next point or [Close/Undo]:	*@35<180*
Specify next point or [Close/Undo]:	*Enter*

■ Complete the remainder of the building by using the same **INQUIRY/ID Point** command and drawing the lines relative to the **ID** points.

The City & Guilds documentation does not specify the size of the square in the upper right corner. I have assumed a dimension of **10.6** for both sides as shown in Figure 1.7, but check with your tutor on this.

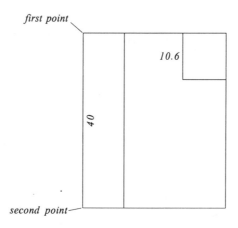

Figure 1.7 *The building outline*

3.7
Entering the Number 23

To insert the number **23** in the building

- Set the text style to **CGMAIN** by using **FORMAT/Text Styles** and clicking on the **CGMAIN** Style Name.

- Use **DRAW/Text/Single Line Text** with a **middle** alignment at coordinates **105, 217**.

Command:	*_dtext*
Current text style: "CGMAIN" Text height: 3.0000	
Specify start point of text or [Justify/Style]:	*m (for middle alignment)*
Specify middle point of text:	*105, 217*
Specify height <3.0000>:	*5*
Specify rotation angle of text <0>:	*Enter*
Enter text:	*23 Enter*
Enter text:	*Enter*

3.8

Drawing the Hatch Pattern

- Firstly, make the layer **Hatch** the **Current** layer.
- Use **DRAW/ Hatch** to create a **User-defined** hatch pattern with spacings of **2** and angle of **45°,** and **4** and angle **135°** respectively as shown in Figure 1.8.

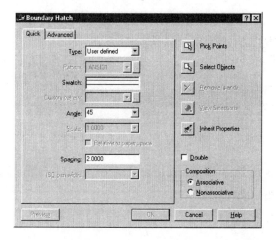

Figure 1.8 *The Boundary Hatch dialogue box with User-defined pattern*

- Hatch the areas with the **Pick Points** option completing the more closely spaced hatched areas first as shown in Figure 1.9.
- Use **Preview** before clicking on **OK** to ensure that it is correct.

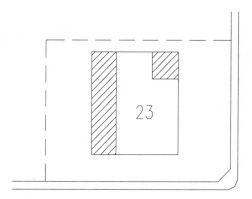

Figure 1.9 *The Building Plan with partially finished hatching*

- Complete the hatching as shown in Figure 1.10 using the same procedure as above.

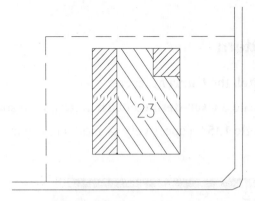

Figure 1.10 *The completed Building Plan*

3.9
Drawing the Arrow

The easiest way to draw this is to draw the circle and arrow and use the **MODIFY/Rotate** command to turn the objects through 27°.

- Make layer **0** the **Current** layer.
- **Draw** the circle with centre coordinates of **45, 265**.
- Use the **Snap to Quadrant** to draw the arrow shape as shown in Figure 1.11.
- Use **Modify/Rotate** to rotate the objects through 27°.

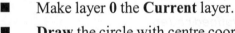

Command: **_rotate**
Current positive angle in UCS: ANGDIR=counterclockwise ANGBASE=0
Select objects: Specify opposite corner: **4 found** *(select the circle and arrow)*
Select objects: **Enter**
Specify base point: **_cen of** *(pick the centre of the circle)*
Specify rotation angle or [Reference]:   **27**

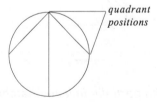

quadrant
positions

Figure 1.11 *The arrow and circle before being rotated*

3.10
Drawing the Key Shaped Object

The easiest way to draw the key-shaped object is to draw it 'down' the page as shown in Figure 1.12 and **MODIFY/Rotate** the finished drawing.

- Use **TOOLS/Drafting Settings** to set the **Grid** and **Snap** to a value of **5** and turn **On**.
- Draw the **Circle** at the required co-ordinate position of **300, 230**.
- Draw an **Inscribed Polygon** with **6** sides, radius **30** and the same centre point as the circle.
- **MODIFY/Explode** the polygon.
- Draw a temporary line from the **MIDpoint** of the bottom line of the polygon with polar co-ordinates of **@50<270** as shown in Figure 1.12.
- **MODIFY/Offset** this line on both sides with a distance of **10**.
- Turn **Snap Off**.
- **MODIFY/Break** the horizontal line between the two outer vertical lines.
- **MODIFY/Fillet** the horizontal broken line of the polygon and the 2 outer vertical lines with a radius of **3** as shown in Figure 1.12.
- Use **DRAW/Arc/Start, End, Radius** to draw the arc at the bottom of the key and draw from the points as shown Figure 1.12.

Remember that arcs are always drawn in an anti-clockwise direction. If you use the arc button as shown on the left, this is the **Arc/Start, Center, End** option and does not ask for a radius.

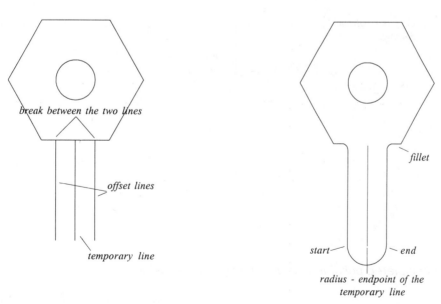

Figure 1.12 *The Key-shaped object drawn down the page*

- **Draw** the angled square as shown in Figure 1.13 starting from the end of the construction line and use polar co-ordinates -
  @8<45
  @8<135
  @8<225
  @8<315

- **Erase** the construction line.

3.11
Drawing the Break Lines

We can draw the break lines with the **DRAW/Polyline** command and as there is no specified starting and finishing point we can use the **Snap to Nearest** to start and finish the line as shown in Figure 1.13.

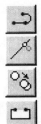

- Use **DRAW/Polyline** to start and finish the line from a start and finish point **Nearest** as shown in Figure 1.13. Remember to set the **Polyline** width to **0**.
- Use the **MODIFY/Copy** command to repeat the object downwards.
- **MODIFY/Break** the two vertical lines between the 2 polylines by using **Snap to Intersection** of the polylines and the vertical lines as shown in Figure 1.13.

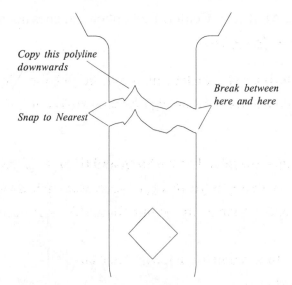

Copy this polyline downwards

Break between here and here

Snap to Nearest

Figure 1.13 *The completed polylines after Copying and Breaking*

3.12
Drawing the Centre Lines

- Make the **Centre** layer the **Current** layer.
- Ensure that **Grid** and **Snap** are **On**.
- Using **FORMAT/Linetype** and in the **Linetype Manager** dialogue box click on **Show Details** and make the **Current Object Scale** of the linetype around **3**.
- Utilising the **Grid** and **Snap**, **Draw** the **2** centrelines as required.
- **Draw** the small line from the **Endpoint** of the angled square
- Use the **MODIFY/Rotate** command to turn the drawing through **90°** as shown in Figure 1.14, using the **Centre** of the circle as the **base point**.

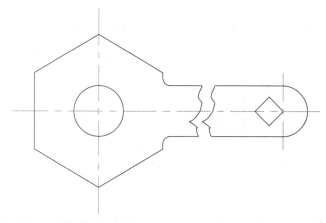

Figure 1.14 *The completed, rotated drawing*

3.13
Drawing the Isometric Bracket

The easiest way to construct the bracket is to draw it to coincide with the grid and snap and use the **MODIFY/Move** command to move the drawing to the required coordinate position of **80, 45** when completed.

- Select **TOOLS/Drafting Settings** and on the **Snap and Grid** tab in the **Drafting Settings** dialogue box under **Snap Style & Type**, select **Isometric Snap**.
- Set **Grid** and **Snap On** and a value of **10** and turn **Snap Off** when necessary.
- Click on **OK**.

You will see the cursor change to an isometric angle (30° and 60°).

- Make layer **0** the **Current** layer.
- Use function key **F5** to set isometric mode to **Top**.

- Use **DRAW/Line** to draw the outline of the bracket using the isometric grid.

- Using **DRAW/Ellipse/Isocircle** draw a circle in the required position and diameter.
- **MODIFY/Copy** this circle downwards by the thickness of the bracket. The grid will aid you with this.
- **MODIFY/Break** the circle at the **INTersections** of the two circles as shown in Figure 1.15.
- Use function key **F5** to set isometric mode to **Left** and repeat drawing the remaining circles in the same way.
- **MODIFY/Move** the drawing to the required coordinates.
- Turn isometric mode back to **Rectangular snap** by using **TOOLS/Drafting Settings** and on the **Snap and Grid** tab in the **Drafting Settings** dialogue box under **Snap Style & Type**, click on **Rectangular Snap**.

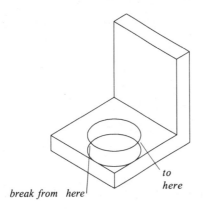
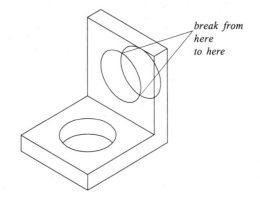

Figure 1.15   *Isometric mode showing the isocircles before being broken.*

3.14

Underlining the Text

Underlining text where the line is associated with the text is easily done by preceding the word with the special control code for underlining text (%%u).

- **Do not try to complete the text by underlining with a drawn line.**
- With **Format/Text Style** ensure that the text style is set to **CGMAIN** with a height of **5** in the **Text Style** dialogue box.
- Using **DRAW/Text/Single Line Text**

```
Command:                                    _dtext
Current text style: "CGMAIN" Text height: 5.0000
Specify start point of text or [Justify/Style]:   pick a start point near the bracket drawing
Specify height <5.0000>:                     Enter
Specify rotation angle of text <0>:          Enter
Enter text:                                  %%uBRACKET  Enter
Enter text:                                  Enter
```

3.15
Drawing the Factory Logo

The factory logo is created with 3 triangular solid filled areas and 3 polylines. We will use the **MOVE** command to move the completed drawing to its required coordinates of **180, 130** after completion.

- Before starting to draw, use **FORMAT/Point Style** to check that the point mode is set to a mode which you can click on when drawn. The cross (X) point style is appropriate.
- Use **DRAW/Polyline** to draw a **Polyline** with the required line thickness of **1.5** using **Grid** and **Snap** if you require.

- **MODIFY/Offset** the line twice upwards with an offset distance of **10**.
- Use **DRAW/Point/Divide** to place point markers on the top line and divided into 3 segments. You will see the marker points appear as crosses.
- Use **DRAW/Surfaces/2D Solid** to produce the triangles, with the first point at the **ENDpoint** of the left hand edge as shown in Figure 1.16

Command:	**Solid**
Specify first point:	**_endp of** *(Snap to endpoint of the polyline for start of 1st triangle)*
Specify second point:	**@10.75<90** *(gives the height of the triangle)*
Specify third point:	**node** *of (**pick** the cross-gives the hypotenuse of the triangle)*
Specify fourth point or <exit>:	**Enter**
Specify third point:	**Enter**

- Repeat the operation for the 2 remaining triangles. For the third point of the 3rd triangle, use **Snap to Endpoint** of the polyline as shown in Figure 1.16.

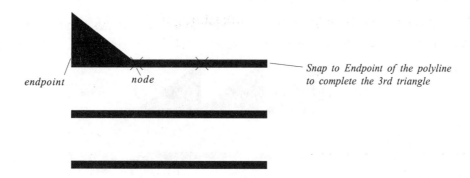

Figure 1.16 *The Factory Logo with the point markers and first triangle completed*

3.16

Placing the Filled Triangles on Top of the Polyline

To place the 3 triangles on top of the polyline

- ■ Use **MODIFY/Move** to move the triangles upwards by half the thickness of the polyline (0.75) using **object snaps**.

- ■ **MODIFY/Erase** the three point crosses.

3.17

Fitting the Text Between the Polylines

- ■ Change the **GRID** and **SNAP** values to **2** with **TOOLS/Drafting Settings**.
- ■ To insert the text use **DRAW/Text/Single Line Text** and set the **Style** to **CGMAIN** with a height of **4**.

- ■ Use the **Fit** option to place the text between the required points, snapping to the grid as shown in Figure 1.17.

Command:	*_dtext*
Current text style: "CGMAIN" Text height: 5.0000	
Specify start point of text or [Justify/Style]:	*F (for fit) Enter*
Specify first endpoint of text baseline:	*(snap to the gridpoint in line with the start of the polyline)*
Specify second endpoint of text baseline:	*(snap to the gridpoint in line with the other end*
of	*the polyline)*
Specify height <5.0000>:	*4*
Enter text:	*FACTORY DESIGN Enter*
Enter text:	*Enter*

- ■ Repeat for the second line of text.

- ■ Use **MODIFY/Move** to transfer the drawing to its coordinates of **180, 130**.

Snap to the grid in line with the end of the polyline

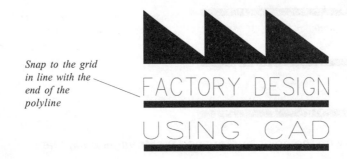

Figure 1.17 *The completed Factory Logo*

3.18

Importing Selected Text

To import the pre-prepared text file

- Use **DRAW/Text/Multiline Text**.

- You will be first asked to specify the text boundary window location and the **Multiline Text Editor** dialogue box will appear as shown in Figure 1.18.

- Ensure that the **Properties** are the **CGMAIN** style with a **Character** height of **5**, a **Justification** of **TL** (Top Left) with **no wrap width** as shown in Figure 1.18.
- Click on **Import Text** to locate the pre-prepared text file.
- Click on **OK** to place the text.

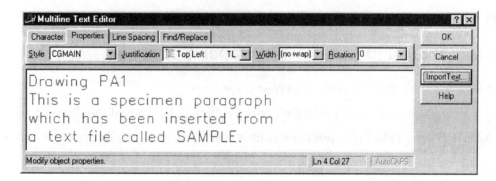

Figure 1.18   *The Multiline Text Editor dialogue box*

3.19

Zooming to Half Scale of Paper Space

Scaling views relative to **Paper Space** establishes a consistent scale for each displayed view in a viewport.

- Use **VIEW/Zoom/Scale** and enter **0.5xp.** The drawing will appear to shrink.

Command: **'_zoom**
All/Center/Dynamic/Extents/Previous/Scale(X/XP)/Window/<Realtime>:   *_s (for scale)*
Enter a scale factor (nX or nXP):   *.5xp*

- Change to **Paper Space**.
- Use **MODIFY/Move** to move the existing viewport by clicking on the cyan coloured border and dragging to its required position.

3.20

Creating a Second Viewport in Paper Space

- Make the layer **PSvports** the **Current** layer.
- To create a second viewport in the bottom right hand corner of the drawing use **VIEW/Viewports/1viewport** and simply specify the diagonally opposite corners.

The whole of the **Model Space** drawing will appear in this viewport.

- Change to **Model Space**.
- Use **VIEW/Zoom/Scale** and enter **1xp**.
- The drawing will zoom and you will need to use **VIEW/ Pan/Realtime** to locate the Building Plan in the viewport.

3.21

Adding the Text Note

- Make layer **0 Current**.
- Ensure that **Paper Space** is active.
- Use **Draw/Text/Single Line Text** to place the text note ensuring that **CGMAIN** is the text style with a height of **3**.

3.22
Freezing the PSVports Layer

- Use **FORMAT/Layer** to make layer **0** the **Current** layer.
- Freeze the **PSVports** layer and the drawing should appear as shown in the required drawing City & Guilds Figure PA1-6.

3.23
Saving the Finished Drawing

To save the drawing

- Use **FILE/Save As** and save the completed project to your floppy disk.

If you use **File/Save** AutoCAD will perform a quick save to the folder that you have been saving to during the project.

3.24
Plotting the Drawing

To plot the drawing

- Use **FILE/Plot** and the **Plot** dialogue box will appear.
- In the **Plot Settings** tab enter a plot scale of **1:1** and **Landscape** drawing orientation as shown in Figure 1.19.
- Use a **Full Preview** to view the drawing before printing.

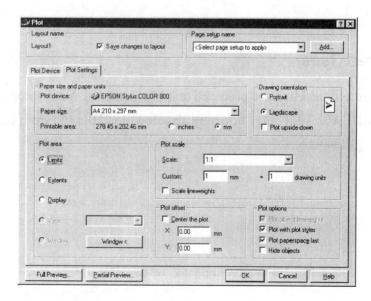

Figure 1.1 *The Plot dialogue box*

PA 4351-01-02

Target Drawing

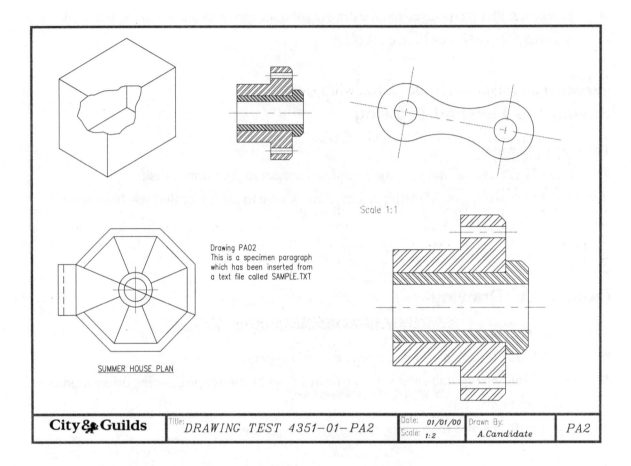

Drawing PA02
This is a specimen paragraph
which has been inserted from
a text file called SAMPLE.TXT

Scale 1:1

SUMMER HOUSE PLAN

City & Guilds	Title: DRAWING TEST 4351-01-PA2	Date: 01/01/00	Drawn By:	PA2
		Scale: 1:2	A.Candidate	

Pre-prepared files

To complete this assignment a pre-prepared text file is needed. Your tutor will provide you with the pre-prepared **'PA02.TXT'** file. You may also download the file from the publisher's website at www.payne-gallway.co.uk.

3.2

Creating a new Drawing with Template Drawing CG-TDPA

- ■ Execute the AutoCAD software and the **Start Up** dialogue box will appear.
- ■ Click on **Use a Template** as shown in Figure 2.1.
- ■ Click on **Browse**.

The **Select a Template file** dialogue box will appear.

- ■ Search for the location of the folder **CGTEMPS** which contains the template file **CG-TDPA.dwt**.
- ■ Click on this filename.
- ■ Click on **Open** to open the template drawing.

As the template drawing was saved in **Paper Space** mode, it should still open in that mode.

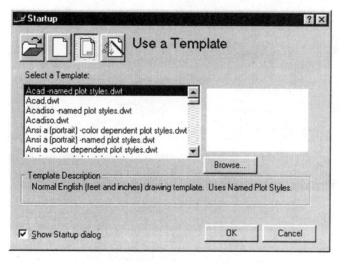

Figure 2.1. The Start Up dialogue box

3.3

Setting the Current Layer to 0

- ■ To set layer **0** as the current layer, in the **Layer Properties Manager** dialogue box click on the layer name **0**.
- ■ Click on **Current**.
- ■ Click on **OK**.

3.4

Completing the Title Bar

To complete the title bar text we must use the **CGITALIC** text style.

To set CGITALIC as the Current Text Style

- Use **FORMAT/Text Style** and the **Text Style** dialogue box will appear as shown in Figure 2.2.

- Click on the **Style Name** pull-down and click on the name **CGITALIC**. The Font Name **Italic.shx** and a width factor of **1** should be loaded.

- Click on **Close** to close the dialogue box.

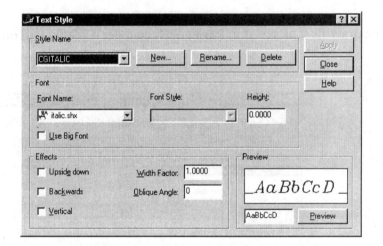

Figure 2.2 *The Text style dialogue box*

Entering the Drawing Number

Before entering the text it will be advisable to enlarge the title bar with the **VIEW/Zoom/Window** command.

We will enter the title and the drawing number first with a text height of 3.5. The drawing number must be in the middle of the box. To ensure this we can draw a temporary line across the middle of the box from the **Midpoint** of line 1, **Perpendicular** to line 2 and then place the text **PA2** as shown in Figure 2.3.

To place the text we will use the **middle** alignment option using the **Midpoint** of the temporary line to place the text exactly in the middle of the box.

■ Use the **DRAW/Line** command to draw the temporary line

Command: _line Specify next point: **_mid of** *(pick the Midpoint of line 1)*
Specify next point: **_per to** *(pick Perpendicular to line 2)*
Specify next point: **Enter**

■ Use **DRAW/Text/Single Line Text** to enter the words **PA2**.

Command: **_dtext**
Current text style: "CGITALIC" Text height: 0.2000
Specify start point of text or [Justify/Style]:   **m** *(for middle alignment)*
Specify middle point of text: **_mid of** *(pick the midpoint of the temporary*
                                                      line)

Specify height <0.2000>:   **3.5**
Specify rotation angle of text <0>:   **Enter**
Enter text: **PA1 Enter**
Enter text: **Enter**

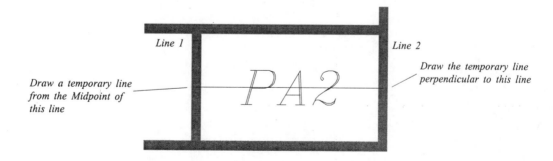

Figure 2.3 *The drawing number box showing the construction line before being erased*

■ **MODIFY/Erase** the temporary line.

■ To enter the title, repeat the above **DRAW/Text/Single Line Text** command but pick a start point as shown in Figure 2.4.

Command:	*_dtext*
Current text style: "CGITALIC" Text height: 3.500	
Specify start point of text or [Justify/Style]:	***pick** a start point for the letter 'D' of Drawing*
Height <3.5000>:	***Enter***
Rotation angle <0>:	***Enter***
Text:	***DRAWING TEST 4351-01-PA2** (Enter)*
Text:	***Enter***

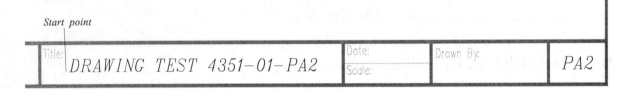

Start point

Figure 2.4 *The partly finished PA2 title block*

■ Repeat the **DRAW/Text/Single Line Text** command to complete the **Date, Scale** and **Drawn By** details but with text heights of **2** and **2.5** respectively.

■ **Zoom/All** when completed.

3.5
Drawing the Isometric Box

The easiest way is to draw the box to coincide with the grid and snap and use the **MODIFY/Move** command to move the drawing to the required coordinate position of **40, 185** when completed.

- Change the drawing mode to **Model Space** by clicking on the **Paper** Button.
- The isometric box can be drawn easily by using **TOOLS/Drafting Settings** and on the **Snap and Grid** tab in the **Drafting Settings dialog box** under **Snap Style & Type**, select **Isometric Snap**.
- Set **Grid** and **Snap** values to **10**.
- Click on **OK**.

You will see the cursor change to an isometric angle (30° and 60°).

- Use **DRAW/Line** to complete the isometric box, in any part of the drawing, using the **Grid** and **Snap** to aid you.

3.6
Drawing the Jagged Edge

- Turn **Snap Off**.

- Use **DRAW/Polyline** with a width of **0** to draw the jagged edge starting at the **Nearest** point as shown in Figure 2.5 and approximate the shape of the jagged edge.

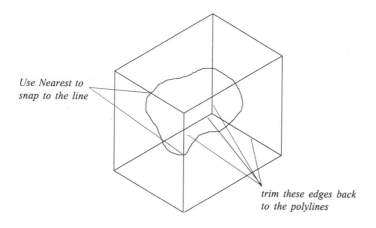

Figure 2.5 The Isometric box before the isometric lines are trimmed back to the polylines

■ As you approach the vertical or the isometric lines use **Nearest** again to snap to the line.

■ When you approach your start point use **C** (for close) to finish on your starting point.

■ To create the effect of a cutaway use the **MODIFY/Trim** command and trim the edges back to the vertical and isometric lines as shown in Figure 2.6.

■ **MODIFY/Move** the drawing to the required coordinates.

The drawing will overlap the border but do not worry about this as when the drawing is scaled relative to **Paper Space** in Objective 3.17 it will appear within the boundary.

■ Turn isometric mode back to **Rectangular snap** by using **TOOLS/Drafting Settings** and on the **Snap and Grid** tab in the **Drafting Settings** dialogue box under **Snap Style & Type**, click on **Rectangular Snap**.

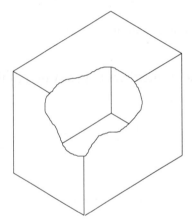

Figure 2.6 The completed Isometric box

3.7
Drawing the Summer House Plan

This exercise requires the use of drawing a polygon with 8 sides, the use of 3 linetypes all on the same layer, various lines, 2 circles and lastly, underlined text. The center of the circles must be at coordinate values **68, 97** but we will draw the plan to align with the grid and move it to the coordinates as the last action.

- Turn **Grid On** with a suitable value.
- Use **DRAW/Circle** to draw the two circles with the centres at a gridpoint.
- Use **DRAW/Polygon** to draw an **inscribed** Polygon with **8** sides and the same centre point as the circles.
- **MODIFY/Offset** the polygon outwards by **7**.
- Use **DRAW/Line** to draw a line from the **Centre** of the circle to one **Intersection** of the inner polygon as shown in Figure 2.7.
- **MODIFY/Trim** the line back to the edge of the outer circle as shown.
- Use **MODIFY Array/Polar** to array the trimmed line with eight objects and traversing **360°**.
- **MODIFY/Extend** the two arrayed lines to the outer polygon.

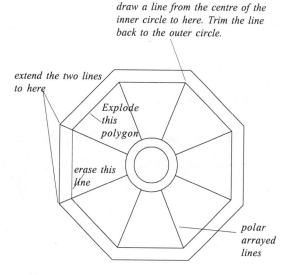

draw a line from the centre of the inner circle to here. Trim the line back to the outer circle.

extend the two lines to here

Explode this polygon

erase this line

polar arrayed lines

Figure 2.7 *The partly completed Summer House Plan*

- Use **MODIFY/Explode** to separate the inner polygon into separate objects in order for us to **MODIFY/Erase** the vertical line on the inner polygon as shown in Figure 2.7.

- Use **MODIFY/Explode** to separate the outer polygon into separate objects in order for us to **MODIFY/Offset** the vertical line on the inner polygon as shown in Figure 2.7.

- **MODIFY/Offset** the outer vertical line as shown in Figure 2.8, by a distance of **11** and **16** respectively.

- Use **DRAW/Line** to connect the outer vertical line with the edge of the outer polygon as shown in Figure 2.8.

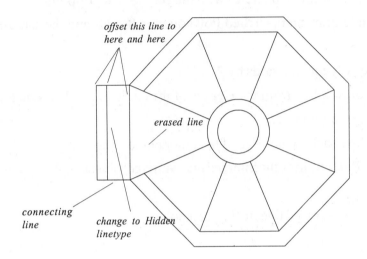

Figure 2.8 *The partly completed Summer House Plan with the 2 lines offset*

3.8

Using an Appropriate Linetype

We need to change the inner line to a broken style and for this we first need to load the linetype by using **FORMAT/Linetype** and the **Linetype Manager** dialogue box will appear as shown in Figure 2.9.

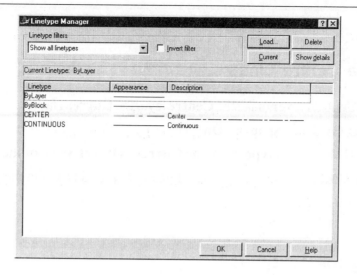

Figure 2.9 *The Linetype Manager dialogue box*

- **Load** the **Hidden** linestyle.

- Use **MODIFY/Properties** to change the linetype from **Continuous** to **Hidden**. The **Properties** dialogue box will appear as shown in Figure 2.10.

- Select the line to change and **Grips** (small blue squares) will appear on the object.

- On the **Categorized** tab click on **Linetype** as shown in Figure 2.10 and from the drop-down menu select **Hidden**.

- On the **Categorized** tab click on **Linetype Scale** as shown in Figure 2.10 and type a figure between **9** and **12**.

- Close the dialogue box and press **Esc** twice to clear the grips and the linetype is changed.

Figure 2.10 *The Properties dialogue box*

The command **Chprop** executes the same command but through the command line only.

3.9
Drawing the Centre Lines

- With **FORMAT/Layer** make the **Centre** layer the **Current** layer.
- Ensure that **Grid** and **Snap** are **On**.
- Using **FORMAT/Linetype** make the **Current Object Scale** of the linetype around **10**.
- Use **DRAW/Line** to draw the 2 centrelines as required utilising the grid and snap to grid.

3.10
Underlining the Text

Underlining text where the line is associated with the text is easily done by preceding the word with the special control code for underlining text (%%u).

- **Do not try to complete the text by underlining with a drawn line.**
- With **FORMAT/Layer** make layer **0** the **Current** layer.
- With **Format/Text Style** ensure that the text style is set to **CGMAIN** with a height of **5** in the **Text Style** dialogue box.
- Using **DRAW/Text/Single Line Text**

Command:	*_dtext*
Specify start point of text or [Justify/Style]:	*s*
Enter style name or [?] <CGMAIN>:	*Enter*
Current text style: "CGMAIN" Text height: 5.0000	
Specify start point of text or [Justify/Style]:	*pick a start point near the bracket*
drawingSpecify height <5.0000>:	*Enter*
Specify rotation angle of text <0>:	*Enter*
Enter text:	*%%uSUMMER HOUSE PLAN Enter*
Enter text:	*Enter*

- Use the **MODIFY/Move** command to move the Summer House Plan using the **Intersection** of the centre lines to the required coordinates of **68, 97**. The drawing will overlap the drawing boundary but do not worry about this as when the drawing drawing is scaled relative to **Paper Space** in Objective 3.17 it will be in its correct position.

3.11

Drawing the Link Drawing

The Link is mainly drawn by using the **Circle** command and **Fillet**ing and **Break**ing the circles. We will draw the Link in a horizontal position, **Move** it to the required coordinates and lastly, **Rotate** it to the required angle.

- Ensure that layer **0** is the **Current** layer.
- Turn **Grid** and **Snap On**.
- Use **DRAW/Circle** to draw the inner right hand circle with its centre snapping to a gridpoint.
- Use **MODIFY/Copy** to copy it **90** units to the left horizontally.
- Repeat for the two larger outer circles.
- Use **MODIFY/Fillet** with a radius of **60** and fillet between the two circles as shown in Figure 2.11.
- **MODIFY/Break** the two circles between the filleted positions. Note that the **First** break points are as shown – always chosen in an anti-clockwise direction.

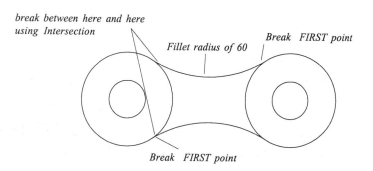

break between here and here
using Intersection

Fillet radius of 60

Break FIRST point

Break FIRST point

Figure 2.11 *The partly completed Link drawing*

3.12
Drawing the Centre Lines

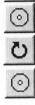

- Make the **Centre** layer the **Current** layer.
- Ensure that **Grid** and **Snap** are **On**.
- Using **FORMAT/Linetype/Show Details** make the **Current Object Scale** of the linetype around **12**.
- Utilising the grid and snap to grid, **Draw** the **3** centrelines as required.
- Use **MODIFY/Move** to move the Link to its coordinates of **320, 272** using the **Centre** of the right hand circle as the base point.
- Use the **MODIFY/Rotate** command to turn the drawing through **-10° (don't forget the minus)** using the **Centre** of the right hand circle as the base point.

The drawing will overlap the drawing boundary but do not worry about this as when the drawing is scaled relative to **Paper Space** in Objective 3.17 it will be in its correct position.

3.13

Drawing the Hub Section

The easiest way to draw the hub is to complete one half and **Mirror** it to complete the drawing and then **Move** it to its required coordinates.

- Make Layer **0** the **Current** layer.
- Ensure that **Grid** and **Snap** are **On** and set to a value of **5**.
- Use **DRAW/Line** to draw only one half of the hub, deducing the dimensions by dividing the diameter dimensions by **0.5** as shown in Figure 2.12.
- Use **MODIFY/Offset** to offset the top line as shown in Figure 2.12 to form a temporary construction line which is also the centreline of the Hub Section.
- Use **MODIFY/Mirror** to copy the drawing, using the temporary line as the mirror points about which the hub is copied upwards.
- Do **not** delete the old objects.

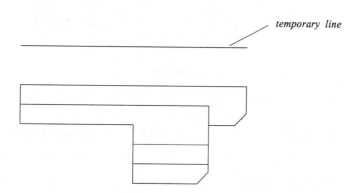

temporary line

Figure 2.12 *One half of the Hub Section*

3.14

Using an Appropriate Hatch Pattern

■ Make **Hatch** the **Current** layer.

■ Use **DRAW/Hatch** with an appropriate pattern (I used **ANSI32**) and a scale of **10** or thereabout as shown in Figure 2.13.

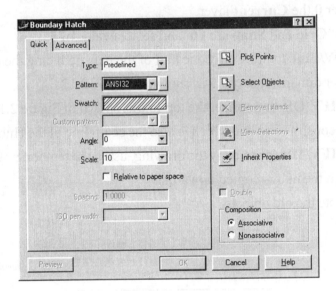

Figure 2.13 *The Boundary Hatch dialogue box*

■ Use the **Pick points** option to select an internal point within the boundary lines as shown in Figure 2.14. You can complete the 'picks' within the one command selection set.

■ Use **Preview** before **Apply**ing it to ensure it is satisfactory.

■ Use the same pattern but with an angle of **90°** and a scale of about half the previous to complete the hatching.

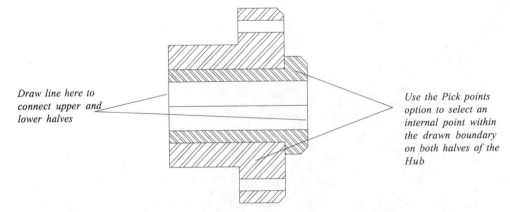

Draw line here to connect upper and lower halves

Use the Pick points option to select an internal point within the drawn boundary on both halves of the Hub

Figure 2.14 *The hatched Hub Section*

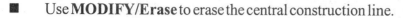

3.15

Drawing the Centrelines

- Use **MODIFY/Erase** to erase the central construction line.
- Make the **Current** Layer **Centre**.
- With **Grid** and **Snap** on and set to **2.5**, draw the centrelines as required.
- Make the **Current** Layer **0**.
- Use **DRAW/Line** to connect the upper and lower halves of the Link as shown in Figure 2.14.
- Lastly, use **MODIFY/Move** to place the Hub at coordinates **166, 235**.

At this stage you will find that the Hub Section collides with the Link which is caused by an error in the City & Guilds documentation.

- Use **MODIFY/Move** to move the drawing to a position advised by your tutor.

3.16

Importing Selected Text

To import the pre-prepared text file

- Make **0** the **Current** layer
- Use **DRAW/Text/Multiline Text**.

You will be first asked to specify the text boundary location and the **Multiline Text Editor** dialogue box will appear as shown in Figure 2.15.

- Ensure that the **Properties** are the **CGMAIN** style with a **Character** height of **5**, a **Justification** of **TL** (Top Left) with **no wrap width** as shown in Figure 2.15.
- Click on **Import Text** to locate the pre-prepared text file.
- Click on **OK** to place the text.

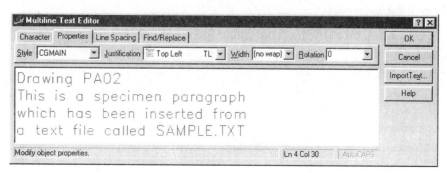

Figure 2.15 *The Multiline Text Editor dialogue box*

3.17
Zooming to Half Scale of Paper Space

Scaling views relative to **Paper Space** establishes a consistent scale for each displayed view in a viewport.

- Use **VIEW/Zoom/Scale** and enter **0.5xp.** The drawing will appear to shrink.

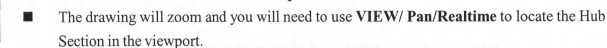

Command: ***'_zoom***
All/Center/Dynamic/Extents/Previous/Scale(X/XP)/Window/<Realtime>:   *_s (for scale)*
Enter a scale factor (nX or nXP):   *.5xp*

- This exercise differs slightly from PA01 in that it does not require you to move the location of the current single viewport but in the finished drawing PA2-6 the viewport does seem to have been moved.

3.18
Creating a Second Viewport in Paper Space

- Change to **Paper Space**.
- Make the layer **PSvports** the **Current** layer.
- To create a second viewport in the bottom right hand corner of the drawing use **VIEW/ Viewports/ 1viewport** and simply specify the diagonally opposite corners.

The whole of the **Model Space** drawing will appear in this viewport.

- Change to **Model Space**.
- Use **VIEW/Zoom/Scale** and enter **1xp**.
- The drawing will zoom and you will need to use **VIEW/ Pan/Realtime** to locate the Hub Section in the viewport.
- Use **MODIFY/Undo** if you do not make the viewport large enough to acommodate the Hub Section.

3.19
Adding the Text Note

MODEL

- Use **FORMAT/Layer** to make layer **0** the **Current** layer.
- Ensure that **Paper Space** is active.
- Use **Draw/Text/Single Line Text** to place the text note ensuring that **CGMAIN** is the text style with a height of **3**.

3.20
Freezing the PSVports Layer

- Ensure that layer **0** is the **Current** layer.
- Freeze the **PSVports** layer and the drawing should appear as shown in the required drawing City & Guilds Figure PA2-6.

3.21
Saving the Finished Drawing

To save the drawing

- Use **FILE/Save As** and save the completed project to your floppy disk.

If you use **File/Save** AutoCAD will perform a quick save to the folder that you have been saving to during the project.

3.22
Plotting the Drawing

To plot the drawing

■ Use **FILE/Plot** and the **Plot** dialogue box will appear.

■ In the **Plot Settings** tab enter a plot scale of **1:1** and **Landscape** orientation as shown in Figure 2.16.

■ Use a **Full Preview** to view the drawing before printing.

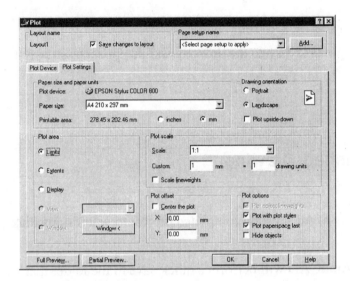

Figure 2.16 The Plot dialogue box

PA 4351-01-03

Target Drawing

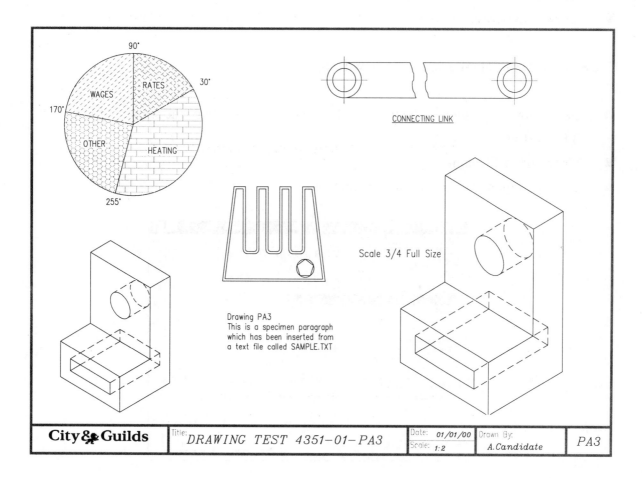

Pre-prepared files

To complete this assignment a pre-prepared text file is needed. Your tutor will provide you with the pre-prepared **'PA03.TXT'** file. You may also download the file from the publisher's website at www.payne-gallway.co.uk.

3.2

Creating a new Drawing with Template Drawing CG-TDPA

■ Execute the AutoCAD software and the **Start Up** dialogue box will appear.

■ Click on **Use a Template** as shown in Figure 3.1.

■ Click on **Browse**.

The **Select a Template file** dialogue box will appear.

■ Search for the location of the folder **CGTEMPS** which contains the template file **CG-TDPA.dwt**.

■ Click on this filename.

■ Click on **Open** to open the template drawing.

Figure 3.1. The Start Up dialogue box

As the template drawing was saved in **Paper Space** mode, it should still open in that mode.

3.3

Setting the Current Layer to 0

■ To set layer **0** as the current layer, in the **Layer Properties Manager** dialogue box click on the layer name **0**.

■ Click on **Current**.

■ Click on **OK**.

3.4

Completing the Title Bar

To complete the title bar text we must use the **CGITALIC** text style.

To set CGITALIC as the Current Text Style

■   Use **FORMAT/Text Style** and the **Text Style** dialogue box will appear as shown in Figure 3.2.

■   Click on the **Style Name** pull-down and click on the name **CGITALIC**. The Font Name **Italic.shx** and a width factor of **1** should be loaded.

■   Click **Close** to close the dialogue box.

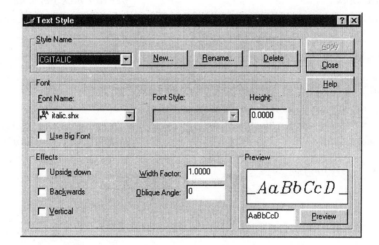

Figure 3.2 *The Text style dialogue box*

Entering the Drawing Number

Before entering the text it will be advisable to enlarge the title bar with the **VIEW/Zoom/Window** command.

We will enter the title and the drawing number first with a text height of **3.5**. The drawing number must be in the middle of the box. To ensure this we can draw a temporary line across the middle of the box from the **Midpoint** of line 1, **Perpendicular** to line 2 and then place the text **PA3** as shown in Figure 3.3.

To place the text we will use the **middle** alignment option using the **Midpoint** of the temporary line to place the text exactly in the middle of the box.

- Use the **DRAW/Line** command to draw the temporary line

  Command: _line Specify next point: ***_mid of** (pick the Midpoint of line 1)*
  Specify next point: ***_per to** (pick Perpendicular to line 2)*
  Specify next point: ***Enter***

- Use **DRAW/Text/Single Line Text** to enter the words **PA3**.

  Command: ***_dtext***
  Current text style: "CGITALIC" Text height: 0.2000
  Specify start point of text or [Justify/Style]:   ***m** (for middle alignment)*
  Specify middle point of text: ***_mid of** (pick the midpoint of the temporary*
  *   line)*
  Specify height <0.2000>:   ***3.5***
  Specify rotation angle of text <0>:   ***Enter***
  Enter text: ***PA3** Enter*
  Enter text: ***Enter***

- **MODIFY/Erase** the temporary line.

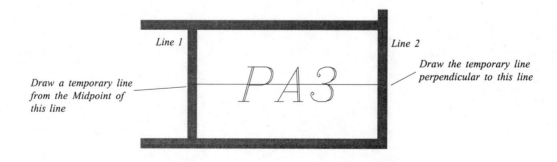

Figure 3.3 *The drawing number box showing the construction line before being erased*

■ To enter the title, repeat the above **DRAW/Text/Single Line Text** command but pick a start point as shown in Figure 3.4.

Command:	*_dtext*
Current text style: "CGITALIC" Text height: 3.500	
Specify start point of text or [Justify/Style]:	**pick** *a start point for the letter 'D' of Drawing*
Height <3.5000>:	***Enter***
Rotation angle <0>:	***Enter***
Text:	***DRAWING TEST 4351-01-PA3*** *(Enter)*
Text:	***Enter***

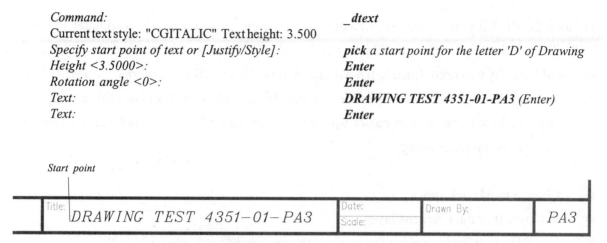

Figure 3.4 *The partly finished PA3 title block*

■ Repeat the **DRAW/Text/Single Line Text** command to complete the **Date**, **Scale** and **Drawn By** details but with text heights of **2** and **2.5** respectively.

■ **Zoom/All** when completed.

3.5
Drawing the Pie Chart

To draw the Pie Chart we need to draw a circle with centre at the required coordinates followed by the lines at the required length. The text style is the **CGMAIN** style which is drawn next followed lastly by two predefined hatch patterns and two user-defined patterns. You will notice that the circle overlaps the boundary of the template border. Don't worry about this as we will be scaling the drawing relative to **Paper Space** in Objective 3.17 and the Pie Chart will appear as required in the target drawing.

- Change to **Model Space**.
- Set layer **0** as the **Current** layer.
- Use **DRAW/Circle** to place the circle at the required coordinates of **42, 252**.
- Use **PAN/Realtime** to pan the drawing so that the circle is within the drawing border.
- Use **DRAW/Line** to draw the four lines from the **Centre** of the circle using polar coordinates to obtain the exact angles of each of the lines as shown in Figure 3.5.

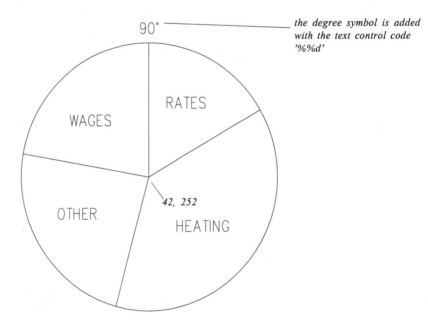

Figure 3.5 *The partially completed Pie Chart*

3.6

Adding the Text Labels

- To draw the text in the four sectors set the style to **CGMAIN**.

- Use **DRAW/Text/Single Line Text** with a height of **5** to enter the required text.

- To enter the angle text around the outside of the circle we can use the text control codes, which in this case is the **'%%d'** code to add a degree symbol as shown in Figure 3.5.

Command:	*_dtext*
Current text style: "CGITALIC" Text height: 2.500	
Command: _dtext Justify/Style/<Start point>:	*s (for Style)*
Style name (or ?) <Standard>:	***CGMAIN** (if CGMAIN is the default style just press **Enter**)*
Justify/Style/<Start point>:	***pick a start point***
Height <2.5000>:	***5*** *Enter*
Rotation angle <0>:	***Enter***
Text:	***90%%d*** *Enter*
Text:	***Enter***

3.7
Drawing the Hatch Patterns

We are required to draw 4 hatch patterns, 2 which are user-defined and 2 which are pre-defined.

- Make layer **Hatch** the **Current** layer.
- Use **DRAW/Hatch** to create a user-defined hatch pattern for **Wages** with a spacing of **3.5** and an angle of **45°** as shown in Figure 3.6.
- Use **Pick Points** and select the internal point by clicking anywhere in the sector. Use **Preview** before **Apply**ing it to ensure it is satisfactory.
- Use the same user-defined hatch pattern and method for the **Rates** sector but check the **Double** box to create a cross hatch pattern as shown in Figure 3.6.
- For the **Other** segment use the pre-stored pattern, **Honey**, with a suitable scale (I used **20** for **Honey** and **Brick**) and hatch as before.
- The **Heating** area is the pre-stored **Brick** pattern.

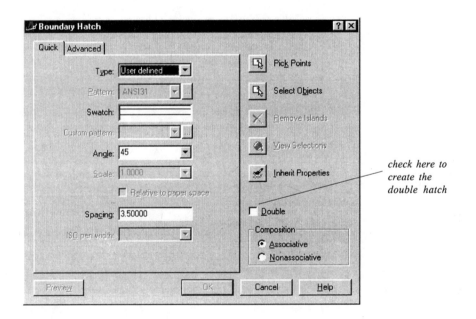

Figure 3.6 The Boundary Hatch dialogue box

3.8
Drawing the Connecting Link

The requirements are to draw the Connecting Link with the left-hand circle centres at coordinates at **226, 290**. However, if we then try to draw the top connecting line, AutoCAD sometimes tells us that it is outside the limits of the drawing. To get over this, pick any point in the drawing to draw the left-hand circles and when completed we will move the drawing to the correct coordinates.

- Make layer **0** the **Current** layer.
- Turn **Grid** and **Snap on** with a suitable value.
- Use **DRAW/Circle** to draw both left-hand circles with centre at a grid point.
- **MODIFY/Copy** the circles **150** units to the right.
- Connect the circles with **DRAW/Line** by using the **Quadrant** (picking the 12 o'clock at the top and 6 o'clock position at the bottom) of the outer circles as shown in Figure 3.7.

Quadrant of the circles(12 o'clock)

Figure 3.7 *The partly completed Connecting Link*

3.9
Drawing the Centre Lines

- Make the **Centre** layer the **Current** layer.
- Ensure that **Snap** is **On** and coincides with the grid.
- Using **FORMAT/Linetype** make the **Current Object Scale** of the linetype about 10.
- Utilising the grid and snap to grid, **Draw** the 2 centrelines as required.

3.10
Underlining the Text

Underlining text where the line is associated with the text is easily done by preceding the word with the special control code for underlining text (%%u).

- Make layer **0** the **Current** layer.
- **Do not try to complete the text by underlining with a drawn line.**
- With **Format/Text Style** ensure that the text style is set to **CGMAIN** with a height of **5** in the **Text Style** dialogue box.
- Using **DRAW/Text/Single Line Text**

Command:	*_dtext*
Specify start point of text or [Justify/Style]:	*s*
Enter style name or [?] <CGMAIN>:	*Enter*
Current text style: "CGMAIN" Text height: 5.0000	
Specify start point of text or [Justify/Style]:	*pick a start point near the bracket*
drawingSpecify height <5.0000>:	*Enter*
Specify rotation angle of text <0>:	*Enter*
Enter text:	*%%uCONNECTING LINK Enter*
Enter text:	*Enter*

3.11
Drawing the Break Lines

We can draw the break lines with the **DRAW/Polyline** command and as there is no specified starting and finishing point we can use the **Snap to Nearest** to start and finish the line as shown in Figure 3.8.

- Ensure that layer **0** is the **Current** layer.
- Turn **Snap Off**.
- Use **DRAW/Polyline** with a **0** width to start and finish the line from a point **Nearest** as shown in Figure 3.8.
- Turn **Ortho On**.
- Use the **MODIFY/Copy** command to repeat the polyline horizontally.
- **MODIFY/Break** the two horizontal lines between the 2 polylines by using **Snap to Intersection** of the polylines and the horizontal lines as shown in Figure 3.8.
- Use **MODIFY/Move** to change the position of the Connecting Link on the drawing so that the centre of the left hand circles are at coordinates **226, 290**.

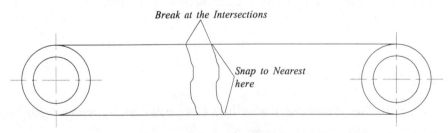

Figure 3.8 *The Connecting link showing the break lines*

3.12

Drawing the Rack

- Set the **Grid** and **Snap** to **10**, both **On**.

- Start by drawing the top right hand line from the required co-ordinatess of **200, 200**. Use the grid to draw the short line lengths of 10 units (alternatively draw the full line of **70** units and use **MODIFY/Break** to create the spaces).

- Draw the bottom horizontal line and join to the ends of the top line.

- Use **DRAW/Line** to draw the left slot downwards by **54.72**, and return up the other side.

- Use **MODIFY/ Fillet** set at a radius of **2**, and add radii at the two bottom corners as shown in Figure 3.9.

- Use **MODIFY/Array/Rectangular** with **1** row, **3** columns and a distance between the columns of **20** to copy the slot.

- Select the slot to array as shown in Figure 3.9 – don't forget to select the radii as well.

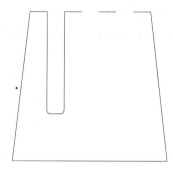

Figure 3.9 *The Rack with the first slot drawn and radii added and ready to array*

To Produce the Inner Flange

The quickest method is to convert the rack outline to a **Polyline** as offsetting individual lines will mean a lot of trimming. (you could, of course, draw the outline with **Polyline** and omit the **Pedit** below).

- Use **MODIFY/Pedit** to convert to a single line polyline

Command: ***pedit***
Select polyline: Select polyline: Select polyline: ***pick*** *one of the lines of the rack*
Object selected is not a polyline
Do you want to turn it into one? <Y>   ***Enter***
Enter an option [Close/Join/Width/Edit vertex/Fit/Spline/Decurve/Ltype gen/Undo]:   ***j*** *(for join)*
Select objects: Specify opposite corner: 22 found   *(selected by window)*
Select objects: ***Enter***

21 segments added to polyline
Enter an option [Open/Join/Width/Edit vertex/Fit/Spline/Decurve/Ltype gen/Undo]: X (for exit)

■ Use **MODIFY/Offset** with a **Distance** of **2** and offset the polyline inwards.

3.13
Drawing the Five-sided Figure

To accurately position the five sided figure is a straightforward operation but will involve accurately positioning the polygon and circle relative to the bottom right hand outside corner of the Rack.

■ Use **TOOLS/Inquiry/ID Point** to establish the coordinates of the bottom corner of the Rack as shown in figure 3.10. This command allows us to specify relative coordinates. You do this by simply picking the **INTersection**.

■ The next command must be the **DRAW/Polygon/Edge** command

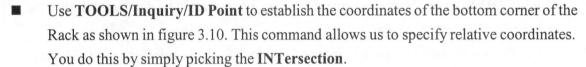

Command: _polygon Enter number of sides <4>:	**5**
Specify center of polygon or [Edge]:	**e** *(for Edge)*
Specify first endpoint of edge:	**@-22,5**
Specify second endpoint of edge:	**@9<0**

■ Use the **DRAW/Circle** command to draw the circle around the polygon using the **3P** option to select the **INTersection**s of 3 sides of the polygon as shown in Figure 3.10.

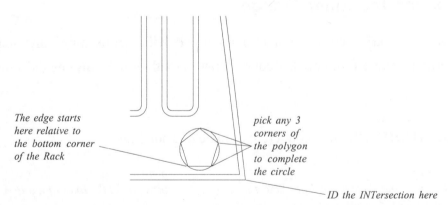

The edge starts here relative to the bottom corner of the Rack

pick any 3 corners of the polygon to complete the circle

ID the INTersection here

Figure 3.10 *The rack showing the positioning of the polygon and circle*

3.14

Drawing the Isometric Block

The easiest method is to draw the block to coincide with the grid and snap and use the **MODIFY/Move** command to move the drawing to the required coordinate position of **31, 9** when completed. We will draw the whole of the block in the same linestyle as shown in Figure 3.11 and then change the properties of the lines that are meant to be hidden, to a broken linestyle.

- Using **TOOLS/Drafting Settings** and on the **Snap and Grid** tab in the **Drafting Settings** dialogue box under **Snap Style & Type**, select **Isometric Snap**.
- Click on **OK**.

You will see the cursor change to an isometric angle (30° and 60°).

- Set **Grid** and **Snap On** and a value of **10**.
- Using **TOOLS/Drafting Settings** turn isometric mode **ON**.
- **Draw** the whole of the block in the same continuous linetype as shown in Figure 3.11.
- Use function key **F5** to set isometric mode to **Left.**
- Using **DRAW/Ellipse/Isocircle** draw two isocircles in the required position and diameter.
- Use **DRAW/Line** to join the two ellipses together with **TANgent** as shown in Figure 3.11.

  This may take a little patience as AutoCAD may tell you that no tangent point can be found – making the **Aperture** size larger may help.

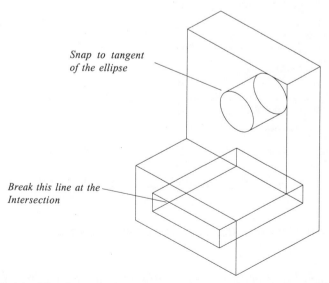

Figure 3.11   The Isometric Block before the hidden lines are changed to a broken style

3.15

Using an Appropriate Linetype

- Before changing the linetype we need to break the line as shown in Figure 3.11 with **MODIFY/Break** so that the whole of that line does not become a broken linestyle.

- Use **FORMAT/Linetype** and the **Linetype Manager** dialogue box will appear.

- **Load** the **Hidden** linestyle and set a **Current Object Scale** of **8-12**.

- Use **MODIFY/Properties** to change the linetype from **Continuous** to **Hidden**.

- The **Properties** dialogue box will appear as shown in Figure 3.12.

- Select the line to change and **Grips** will appear on the object.

- On the **Categorized** tab click on **Linetype** as shown in Figure 3.12.

- From the drop-down menu select **Hidden**.

- Close the dialogue box and press **Esc** twice to clear the grips and the linetype is changed.

- Turn isometric mode back to **Rectangular snap** by using **TOOLS/Drafting Settings** and on the **Snap and Grid** tab in the **Drafting Settings** dialogue box under **Snap Style & Type**, click on **Rectangular Snap**.

Figure 3.12   *The Properties dialogue box*

The command **Chprop** executes the same command but through the command line only.

- Use **MODIFY/Move** to move the whole of the Isometric Block to its required coordinates.

The drawing will overlap the boundary but don't worry as Scaling to Paper Space in Objective 3.17 will confine it within the boundary.

3.16

Importing the Selected Text

To import the pre-prepared text file

- Use **DRAW/Text/Multiline Text**.

You will be first asked to specify the text boundary window location and the **Multiline Text Editor** dialogue box will appear as shown in Figure 3.13.

- Ensure that the **Properties** are the **CGMAIN** style with a **Character** height of **5**, a **Justification** of **TL** (Top Left) with **no wrap width** as shown in Figure 3.13.
- Click on **Import Text** to locate the pre-prepared text file.
- Click on **OK** to place the text.

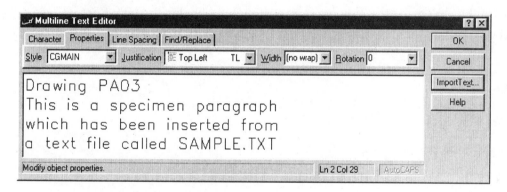

Figure 3.13   *The Multiline Text Editor dialogue box*

3.17

Zooming to Half Scale of Paper Space

Scaling views relative to **Paper Space** establishes a consistent scale for each displayed view in a viewport.

- Use **VIEW/Zoom/Scale** and enter **0.5xp.** The drawing will appear to shrink.

Command: **'_zoom**
All/Center/Dynamic/Extents/Previous/Scale(X/XP)/Window/<Realtime>:   **_s (for scale)**
Enter a scale factor (nX or nXP):   **.5xp**

- Change to **Paper Space**.
- This exercise differs slightly from PA01 in that it does not require you to move the location of the current single viewport but in the finished drawing PA3-6 the viewport does seem to have been moved.

3.18
Creating a Second Viewport in Paper Space

- Make the layer **PSvports** the **Current** layer.
- To create a second viewport in the bottom right hand corner of the drawing use **VIEW/Viewports/1viewport** and simply specify the diagonally opposite corners.

The whole of the **Model Space** drawing will appear in this viewport.

- Change to **Model Space**.
- Use **VIEW/Zoom/Scale** and enter **.75xp**.
- The drawing will zoom and you will need to use **VIEW/ Pan/Realtime** to locate the Isometric Block in the viewport.
- If you haven't made the viewport large enough to display the Hub Section, use **MODIFY/ Undo** to delete the last few actions and start again.

3.19
Adding the Text Note

- Ensure that **Paper Space** is active.
- Make the layer **0** the **Current** layer.
- Use **Draw/Text/Single Line Text** to place the text note ensuring that **CGMAIN** is the text style with a height of **3**.

3.20
Freezing the PSVports Layer

- Ensure that layer **0** is the **Current** layer.
- Freeze the **PSVports** layer and the drawing should appear as shown in the required drawing City & Guilds Figure PA3-6.

3.21
Saving the Finished Drawing

To save the drawing

- Use **FILE/Save As** and save the completed project to your floppy disk.

If you use **File/Save** AutoCAD will perform a quick save to the folder that you have been saving to during the project.

3.22

Plotting the Drawing

To plot the drawing

- Use **FILE/Plot** and the **Plot** dialogue box will appear.
- In the **Plot Settings** tab enter a plot scale of **1:1** and **Landscape** orientation as shown in Figure 3.14.
- Use a **Full Preview** to view the drawing before printing.

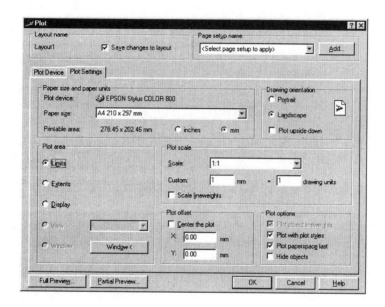

Figure 3.14   *The Plot dialogue box*

PA 4351-01-04

Target Drawing

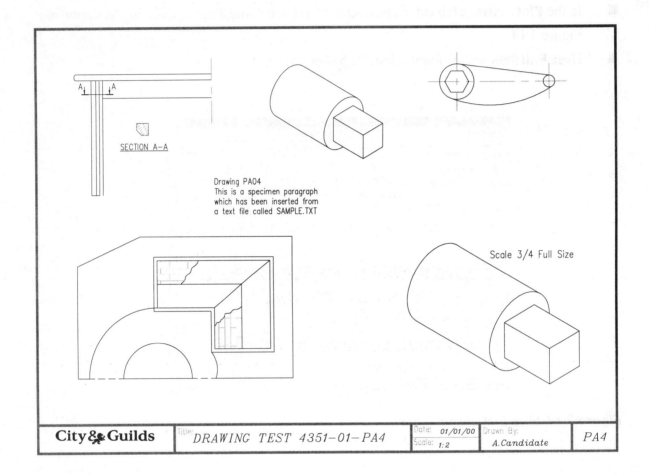

SECTION A-A

Drawing PA04
This is a specimen paragraph
which has been inserted from
a text file called SAMPLE.TXT

Scale 3/4 Full Size

| City & Guilds | Title: DRAWING TEST 4351-01-PA4 | Date: 01/01/00 | Drawn By: | PA4 |
| | | Scale: 1:2 | A.Candidate | |

Pre-prepared files

To complete this assignment a pre-prepared text file is needed. Your tutor will provide you with the pre-prepared '**PA04.TXT**' file. You may also download the file from the publisher's website at www.payne-gallway.co.uk.

3.2

Creating a new Drawing with Template Drawing CG-TDPA

■ Execute the AutoCAD software and the **Start Up** dialogue box will appear.

■ Click on **Use a Template** as shown in Figure 4.1.

■ Click on **Browse**.

The **Select a Template file** dialogue box will appear.

■ Search for the location of the folder **CGTEMPS** which contains the template file **CG-TDPA.dwt**.

■ Click on this filename.

■ Click on **Open** to open the template drawing.

As the template drawing was saved in **Paper Space** mode, it should still open in that mode.

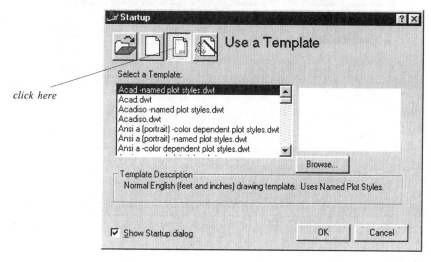

Figure 4.1. The Start Up dialogue box

3.3

Setting the Current Layer to 0

■ To set layer **0** as the current layer, in the **Layer Properties Manager** dialogue box click on the layer name **0**.

■ Click on **Current**.

■ Click on **OK**.

3.4
Completing the Title Bar

To complete the title bar text we must use the **CGITALIC** text style.

To set CGITALIC as the Current Text Style

■ Use **FORMAT/Text Style** and the **Text Style** dialogue box will appear as shown in Figure 4.2.

■ Click on the **Style Name** pull-down and click on the name **CGITALIC**. The Font Name **Italic.shx** and a width factor of **1** should be loaded.

■ Click on **Close** to close the dialogue box.

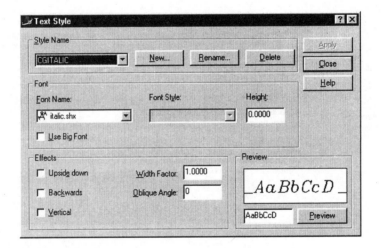

Figure 4.2 *The Text style dialogue box*

Entering the Drawing Number

Before entering the text it will be advisable to enlarge the title bar with the **VIEW/Zoom/Window** command.

We will enter the title and the drawing number first with a text height of 3.5. The drawing number must be in the middle of the box. To ensure this we can draw a temporary line across the middle of the box from the **Midpoint** of line 1, **Perpendicular** to line 2 and then place the text **PA1** as shown in Figure 4.3.

To place the text we will use the **middle** alignment option using the **Midpoint** of the temporary line to place the text exactly in the middle of the box.

- Use **VIEW/Zoom/Window** to enlarge the area.

- Use the **DRAW/Line** command to draw the temporary line

Command: _line Specify next point:	***_mid of** (pick the Midpoint of line 1)*
Specify next point:	***_per to** (pick Perpendicular to line 2)*
Specify next point:	***Enter***

- Use **DRAW/Text/Single Line Text** to enter the words **PA4**

Command:	***_dtext***
Current text style: "CGITALIC" Text height: 0.2000	
Specify start point of text or [Justify/Style]:	***m** (for middle alignment)*
Specify middle point of text:	***_mid of** (pick the midpoint of the temporary line)*
Specify height <0.2000>:	***3.5***
Specify rotation angle of text <0>:	***Enter***
Enter text:	***PA4** Enter*
Enter text:	***Enter***

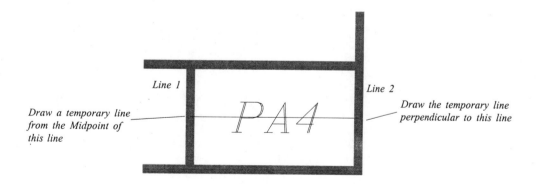

Figure 4.3 *The drawing number box showing the construction line before being erased*

■ **MODIFY/Erase** the temporary line.

■ To enter the title, repeat the above **DRAW/Text/Single Line Text** command but pick a start point as shown in Figure 4.4.

Command: *_dtext*
Current text style: "CGITALIC" Text height: 3.500
Specify start point of text or [Justify/Style]:   **pick** *a start point for the letter 'D' of Drawing*
Height <3.5000>:   **Enter**
Rotation angle <0>:   **Enter**
Text: **DRAWING TEST 4351-01-PA4** *(Enter)*
Text: **Enter**

■ Repeat the **DRAW/Text/Single Line Text** command to complete the **Date**, **Scale** and **Drawn By** details but with text heights of **2** and **2.5** respectively.

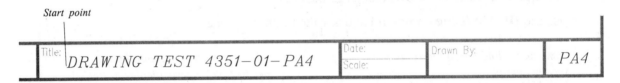

Figure 4.4 *The partly finished PA4 title block*

■ Use **VIEW/Zoom/All** when completed.

3.5

Completing the Table Drawing

The Table is straightforward, but if you start drawing the table leg at the start coordinates of **28, 200** and try to draw the vertical line of **97.4**, AutoCAD may give an error message of **'Outside Limits'**. Therefore, we will draw within the limits and, lastly, move the completed drawing. When the drawing is moved, it will be partly outside the border, but don't be concerned over this as we will be using **Zoom/.5xp** in Objective 3.19 to complete the drawing as required.

- Change the drawing mode to **Model Space** by clicking on the **Paper** button.
- Set layer **0** as the **Current** layer.
- Pick a start point anywhere within the limits.
- Use **DRAW/Line** to start the left hand line of the table leg at a length of **97.4**.
- Use **MODIFY/Offset** to copy this line **4**, **7** and **10** units to the right as shown in Figure 4.5.
- Use **DRAW/Line** to draw a line from the initial start point to the end of the line that was offset by **7** units to form the bottom of the leg as shown in Figure 4.5.
- Use **DRAW/Line** to draw a line 105 units long to the right, from the end of the vertical line you drew first.
- Use **MODIFY/Lengthen** to make this line a total of **120** units long and lengthen to the left.

```
Command:                                        _lengthen
Select an object or [DElta/Percent/Total/DYnamic]:   de (for DElta)
Enter delta length or [Angle] <0.0000>:         15 (this will make the total length of 120 units)
Select an object to change or [Undo]:           pick (pick the horizontal line near its left hand
                                                     end)
Select an object to change or [Undo]:           Enter (the line becomes 120 units long)
```

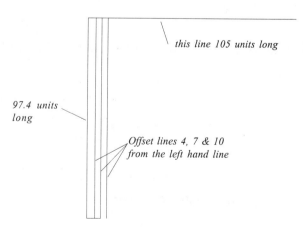

this line 105 units long

97.4 units long

Offset lines 4, 7 & 10 from the left hand line

Figure 4.5 *The Table leg and part of the top before Lengthening and Offsetting*

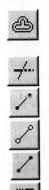

- Use **MODIFY/Offset** to offset this line upwards by **5** and downwards by **15** as shown in Figure 4.6.
- Use **MODIFY/Trim** to cut the line offset downwards by **15** back to the vertical line.
- Use **DRAW/Line** to join this line from the vertical line to the **Endpoint** of the leg as shown in Figure 4.6
- Join the left hand of the table top with **DRAW/ Line**.
- Use **MODIFY/Fillet** with a radius of **2** on the upper and lower edge, as shown in Figure 4.6.

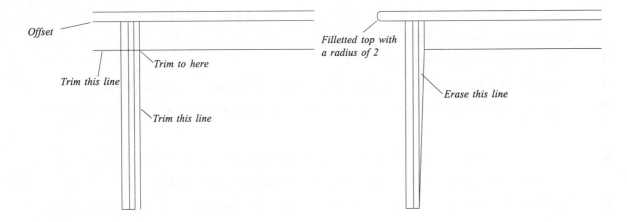

Figure 4.6 *The partly completed table showing the offsetted lines before and after trimming and filletting.*

Drawing the Leg Section

- Turn **Grid** and **Snap** to **On** with a value of **10**.
- Use **DRAW/Rectangle** by specifying the diagonally opposite corners and it is quickly completed.
- Turn **Snap** to **Off**.
- Use **MODIFY/Chamfer** with **first** and **second** distances of **4** as shown in Figure 4.7.

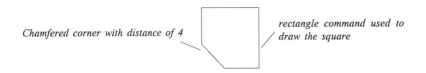

Figure 4.7 *The Table leg cross-section showing the filleted corner*

3.6

Using a Suitable Hatch Pattern

- Make Hatch the **Current** layer.
- Use **DRAW/Hatch** with an appropriate pattern (I used **ANSI31**) and a scale of **10** to **15** or thereabouts as shown in Figure 4.7.
- Use the **Pick points** option to select an internal point within the boundary lines of the square.
- Use **Preview** before clicking **OK** to ensure it is satisfactory.

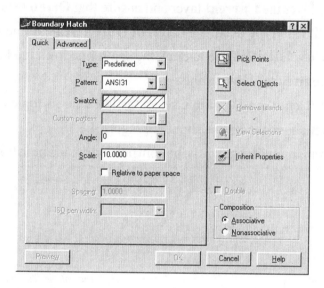

Figure 4.7 *The Boundary Hatch dialogue box*

3.7

Underlining the Text

Underlining text where the line is associated with the text is easily done by preceding the word with the special control code for underlining text (%%u).

- **Do not try to complete the text by underlining with a drawn line.**
- Make layer **0** the **Current** layer.
- With **Format/Text Style** ensure that the text style is set to **CGMAIN** with a height of **5** in the **Text Style** dialogue box.
- Using **DRAW/Text/Single Line Text**

Command: *_dtext*
Specify start point of text or [Justify/Style]:   *s*

Enter style name or [?] <CGMAIN>:	***Enter***
Current text style: "CGMAIN" Text height: 5.0000	
Specify start point of text or [Justify/Style]:	***pick*** *a start point near the bracket*
drawingSpecify height <5.0000>:	***Enter***
Specify rotation angle of text <0>:	***Enter***
Enter text:	***%%uSECTION A-A*** *Enter*
Enter text:	***Enter***

3.8
Drawing the Centre Line

- Make the Centre layer the **Current** layer and ensure that **Ortho** is on.
- Using **FORMAT/Linetype** make the **Current Object Scale** of the linetype around **12**.
- Utilising **Ortho**, use **DRAW/Line** to draw the centreline from the **Endpoint** of the top line to the **Endpoint** of the bottom line.
- Using **MODIFY/Lengthen/DYnamic** select the line near its top end and lengthen it by specifying a point above the line as shown in Figure 4.8.
- Continue the command and lengthen the bottom portion of the line in the same way.

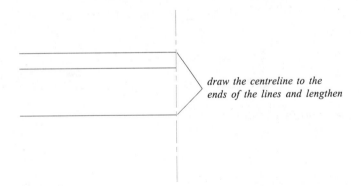

draw the centreline to the ends of the lines and lengthen

Figure 4.8 *The Centre line after lengthening*

3.9
Drawing the Cutting Plane

The cutting plane section line involves using the Polyline command with a uniform width to draw the ends of the horizontal line and a non-uniform width to draw the arrowhead. The arrow can be copied to the other end of the polyline before entering the text in the **CGMAIN** style.

- Make layer **0** the **Current** layer.
- With **Ortho** on, use **DRAW/Line** to draw the horizontal line in the required position with length decided by you.

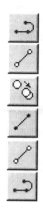

- Using **DRAW/Polyline** with a uniform starting and ending width of around **0.5**, draw a short polyline from the **Endpoint** of the horizontal line.
- **MODIFY/Copy** it to the other end of the horizontal line as shown in Figure 4.9.
- To draw an arrow and with **Ortho** still active, use **DRAW/Line** to draw a short vertical line.
- From the **Endpoint** of the bottom of the short vertical line use **DRAW/Polyline** to draw the arrow head with a starting width of **0**, and an ending width of **1** with length decided by you.

Command:	*_pline*
From point:	*_endp of (pick the bottom of the vertical line)*
Current line-width is 0.0000	
Specify next point or [Arc/Close/Halfwidth/Length/Undo/Width]:	*w*
Specify starting width <0.0000>:	*Enter*
Specify ending width <0.0000>:	*1*
Arc/Close/Halfwidth/Length/Undo/Width/<Endpoint of line>:	*pick a point on the vertical line*
Arc/Close/Halfwidth/Length/Undo/Width/<Endpoint of line>:	*Enter*

- Use **MODIFY/Copy** to copy to the other end of the horizontal line.
- Use **FORMAT/Text Style** to ensure that **CGMAIN** is the style, and type the **'A'**,s in the required position.
- Turn **Ortho Off**.
- Lastly, use **MODIFY/Move** to move the drawing to its coordinates of **28, 200** using the **Intersection** or **Endpoint** of the bottom left hand corner of the leg as the base point.

The drawing will overlap the drawing boundary but do not worry about this as when the drawing is scaled relative to **Paper Space** in Objective 3.19 it will be in its correct position.

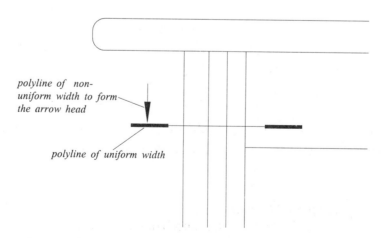

polyline of non-uniform width to form the arrow head

polyline of uniform width

Figure 4.9 *The partly completed section lines and arrow*

3.10

Drawing the Isometric Shaft

The Isometric Shaft presents few problems other than remembering to set to **Isometric** mode. The other slight problem is that when you draw a line tangential to the ellipse AutoCAD has difficulty in locating the tangent. AutoCAD may, on the first pick, give you a wrong tangent point – if so, **Cancel** the command and try again as second time around usually works – also, making the **Aperture** size larger may help. Lastly, it is easier to complete the Isometric Shaft before moving it to its required coordinates which are incorrectly shown as **135, 55**. I moved the finished drawing to **275, 225** but consult your tutor on this.

- The isometric shaft can be drawn easily by using **TOOLS/Drafting Settings** and on the **Snap and Grid** tab in the **Drafting Settings** dialogue box under **Snap Style & Type**, select **Isometric Snap**.
- Set **Grid** and **Snap On** and a value of **10**.
- Click on **OK**.

You will see the cursor change to an isometric angle (30° and 60°).

- Use **Draw/Line** to draw the outline of the block starting at a point decided by yourself.
- Using function key **F5** set the isometric mode to **Right**.

- Using **DRAW/Ellipse/Isocircle** draw an isometric circle with the required position and diameter as shown in Figure 4.10.

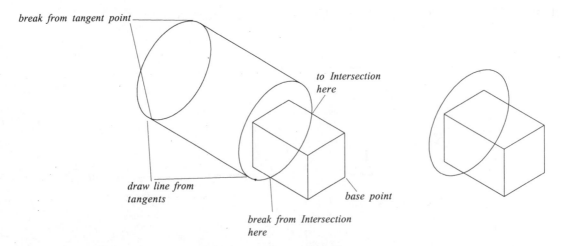

Figure 4.10   *The partly completed Isometric Shaft*

- Draw a second Isocircle (or **MODIFY/Copy** the first one, taking care to locate the second point of displacement **55** units along the isometric axis – using polar coordinates **@55<150**), snapping to its correct position.

- Use **DRAW/Line** to join the two ellipses together by using **TANgent**.

- Use **MODIFY/Break** to break the circles at the **INTersections** as shown in Figure 4.10. **Remember to pick in an anti-clockwise direction.**

- **MODIFY/MOVE** the drawing to coordinates of **275, 225** using the base point as shown in Figure 4.10.

- Turn isometric mode back to **Rectangular snap** by using **TOOLS/Drafting Settings** and on the **Snap and Grid** tab in the **Drafting Settings** dialogue box under **Snap Style & Type**, click on **Rectangular Snap**.

3.11/3.12

Drawing the Belt Drive

To draw the Belt Drive we need to draw two circles (the smaller circle has a radius of **5**, which is missing from the instructions), an inscribed polygon, a line tangential to the two circles and a circle of **100** radius which is broken at the tangents to the two circles. The coordinate position for the circle and polygon centres does clash with the already drawn Isometric Shaft. I used coordinates 320, 260 but check with your tutor on this.

- Ensure that layer **0** is the **Current** layer.
- Make the **Grid** and **Snap** values **5** and turn **On**. This will help later when we draw the centrelines.
- Use **DRAW/Circle** at coordinates **320, 260**.
- Use **DRAW/Polygon/Circumscribed** with **6** sides and **Radius** of **9**.
- Draw the second smaller circle at **400, 260** as shown in Figure 4.11.
- Join the the tops of the circles with **DRAW/LINE** and **TANGential** to each.
- To join the bottoms of the circles use **DRAW/CIRCLE/TTR** (**Tangent,Tangent, Radius**) and choose the tangent points.
- Enter a radius of **100**.
- **MODIFY/Break** the circle at the **INTersections** as shown in Figure 4.11. Remember to pick in an anti-clockwise direction.

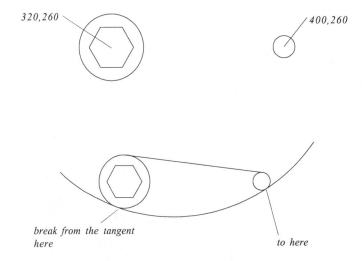

Figure 4.11 *The Belt Drive before breaking the circle*

3.13

Drawing the Centre Lines

■ Make the Centre layer the **Current** layer.

■ Ensure that **Grid** and **Snap** are **On**.

■ Use **FORMAT/Linetype** to make the **Current Object Scale** of the linetype around **12**.

■ Utilising the grid and snap to grid use **DRAW/Line** to draw the **3** centrelines as required.

■ Make layer **0** the **Current** layer.

3.14
Drawing the Site Plan

The Site Plan is completed by drawing the boundary as a rectangle shape and chamfering the corner. The building can be located within the boundary by coordinates relative to the bottom left hand corner of the boundary. The building outline is then offset outwards followed by drawing the roof ridge lines. The driveway arcs centre points are located with coordinates relative to the bottom left hand corner of the boundary again. The bottom boundary line is broken at the arc intersections and the linetype style is changed. The jagged edge lines are polylines and the hatch pattern is a suitably scaled brick pattern. The start coordinates as shown in the instructions are incorrect if you look at the C&G finished drawing PA4-6 so I started the boundary from the bottom left hand corner at coordinates **15, 45** but confirm this with your tutor first.

- Turn **Grid** and **Snap On** and a value of **5** (this is optional).
- Use **DRAW/Line** to start the site boundary at coordinates **15, 45** and draw a rectangle shape **190x120**.
- Use **MODIFY/Chamfer** with a first distance of **25** and second distance of **55** and chamfer the top left corner as shown in Figure 4.12.
- To locate the bottom left hand corner of the building with coordinates relative to the bottom left corner of the boundary use **TOOLS/Inquiry/ID Point** at the **Intersection** of the bottom left hand boundary corner as shown in Figure 4.12 (you could also use the **Tracking** command).
- The next command must be **DRAW/Polyline** with relative coordinates **@70, 60** to locate the inner bottom left hand corner of the building outline and complete the building outline.
- Use **MODIFY/Offset** to offset this polyline outwards by **3** as shown in Figure 4.12.
- For the roof ridge, use **DRAW/Line** to draw the diagonal ridge line.

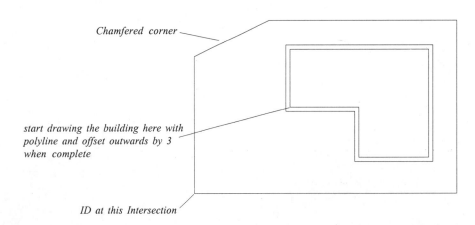

Chamfered corner

start drawing the building here with polyline and offset outwards by 3 when complete

ID at this Intersection

Figure 4.12 *The Site Plan showing the boundary and building outline*

- Use **DRAW/Line** and snap to **MIDpoint** to locate the two other ridge lines as shown in Figure 4.13.

- To draw the larger drive radii, use **DRAW/Arc/Start, Centre, Angle** starting from the inner bottom corner of the building as shown in Figure 4.13. and drawing the **Centre** of the arc **Perpendicular** to the bottom boundary line at an angle of **90°**.

Command: _arc Center/<Start point>:	***_endp of***	*(pick the corner as shown in Figure 4.13)*
Center/End/<Second point>:	***c***	*(for centre)*
Center:	***_per to***	*(the bottom boundary line)*
Angle/Length of chord/<End point>:	***a***	*(for angle)*
Included angle:	***90***	

To locate the centre of the half circle we can use **TOOLS/Inquiry/ID Point** as before at the bottom left hand corner of the boundary as shown in Figure 4.13. Follow this with **DRAW/Arc/Centre Start Angle** for the small radii as shown. Remember to pick in an anti-clockwise direction.

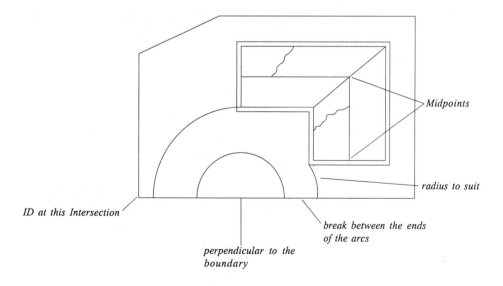

Command:	***id***
Specify Point:	***_int of** pick the bottom left corner of the boundary line*
(coordinates 15, 45)	
Command:	***_arc Center/<Start point>: _c Center: @70,0** (gives the centre point relative to the previous point)*
Start point:	*@30,0 (the radius of the arc and the right hand start point)*
Angle/Length of chord/<End point>: _a Included angle: 180 (draws half a circle)	

- Use **DRAW/Arc/3 points** to draw the arc with radius to suit as shown in Figure 4.13.

Midpoints

radius to suit

ID at this Intersection

break between the ends
of the arcs

perpendicular to the
boundary

Figure 4.13 *The partly completed Site Plan*

■ Use **Nearest** to pick a point on the bottom boundary line, a point about halfway between the boundary and the building and lastly, the bottom corner of the building in that order.

■ Use **MODIFY/Trim** to trim the large arc back to the outer edge of the building.

3.15

Using an Appropriate Linetype

 ■ Use **MODIFY/Break** to break the ends of the arcs at the bottom boundary as shown in Figure 4.13 and the lines between the arcs will be erased.

■ Use **FORMAT/Linetype** and in the **Linetype Manager** dialogue box use **Load** to load the **Hidden** linestyle.

■ Set the **Hidden** style to **Current**.

 ■ Use **DRAW/Line** to draw lines between the ends of the arcs.

■ Set the **Current** linetype back to **Bylayer**.

3.16

Drawing the Jagged Edges

 ■ We can draw the break lines with the **DRAW/Polyline** command and as there is no specified starting and finishing point we can use the **Snap to Nearest** to start, and finish the lines as shown in Figure 4.14.

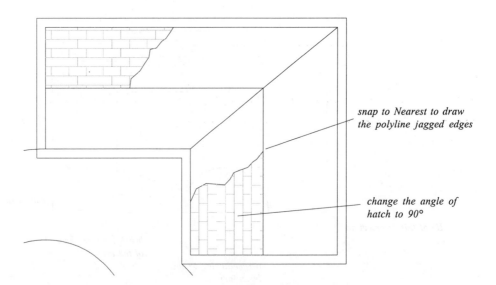

Figure 4.14 The jagged edges and hatching of the roof

3.17
Using an Appropriate Hatch Pattern

We are required to draw a hatch pattern, which is the pre-drawn **Brick** pattern.

- Make layer **Hatch** the **Current** layer.
- Use **DRAW/Hatch** to select the Brick pattern with a scale of **2** or **3** as shown in Figure 4.15.
- Use **Pick Points** and select the internal point of the horizontal part of the roof by clicking anywhere in the sector.
- For the vertical part of the roof, change the angle of the pattern to **90°** as shown in Figure 4.14.
- Use **Preview** before clicking on **OK** to ensure it is satisfactory.

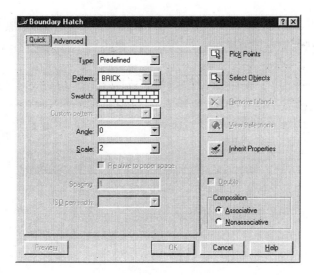

Figure 4.15 *The Boundary Hatch dialogue box with Brick pattern*

3.18
Importing Selected Text

■ Make layer **0** the **Current** layer.

To import the pre-prepared text file

■ Use **DRAW/Text/Multiline Text**.

You will be first asked to specify the text window boundary location and the **Multiline Text Editor** dialogue box will appear as shown in Figure 4.16.

■ Ensure that the **Properties** are the **CGMAIN** style with a **Character** height of **5**, a **Justification** of **TL** (Top Left) with **no wrap width** as shown in Figure 4.16.

■ Click on **Import File** to locate the pre-prepared text file.

■ Click on **OK** to place the text.

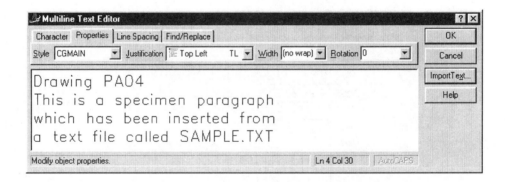

Figure 4.16 *The Multiline Text Editor dialogue box*

3.19

Zooming to Half Scale of Paper Space

Scaling views relative to **Paper Space** establishes a consistent scale for each displayed view in a viewport. To do this we can use **VIEW/Zoom/Scale** and enter **0.5xp.** The drawing will appear to shrink.

> *Command:*   *'_zoom*
> *Specify corner of window, enter a scale factor (nX or nXP), or [All/Center/Dynamic/Extents/*
> *Previous/Scale/Window] <real time>:*   *_s*
> *Enter a scale factor (nX or nXP):*   *.5xp*

- Change to **Paper Space**.

This exercise differs slightly from PA01 in that it does not require you to move the location of the current single viewport but in the finished drawing PA4-6 the viewport does seem to have been moved.

3.20

Creating a Second Viewport in Paper Space

- Make the layer **PSvports** the **Current** layer.
- To create a second viewport in the bottom right hand corner of the drawing use **VIEW/ Floating Viewports/1 viewport** and you will be asked to specify the diagonally opposite corners. The whole of the **Model Space** drawing will appear in this viewport.

- Change to **Model Space**.
- Use **VIEW/Zoom/Scale** and enter **.75xp**.
- The drawing will zoom and you will need to use **VIEW/ Pan/Realtime** to locate the Building Plan in the viewport.

3.21

Adding the Text Note

- Make the layer **0** the **Current** layer.
- With **Paper Space** active use **Draw/Text/Single Line Text** to place the text note ensuring that **CGMAIN** is the style with a height of **3**.

3.22
Freezing the PSVports Layer

■ Use **FORMAT/Layer** to make layer **0 Current** and freeze the **PSVports** layer and the drawing should appear as shown in the required drawing City & Guild Figure PA4-6.

3.23
Saving the Finished Drawing

■ To save the drawing use **FILE/Save as** and save the completed project to your floppy disk.

If you use **File/Save** AutoCAD will perform a quick save to the folder that you have been saving to during the project.

3.24
Plotting the Drawing

■ To plot the drawing use **FILE/Plot** and the **Plot** dialogue box will appear.
■ Enter a scale of **1:1** as shown in Figure 4.17 and a **Landscape** orientation.
■ Use a **Full Preview** to view the drawing before printing.

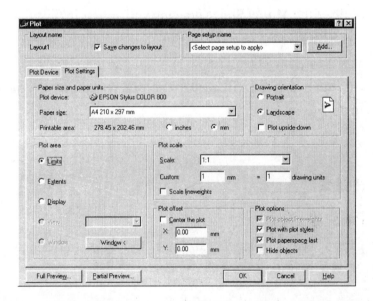

Figure 4.17   *The Plot dialogue box*

PA 4351-01-05

Target Drawing - Part 1 - PA5A

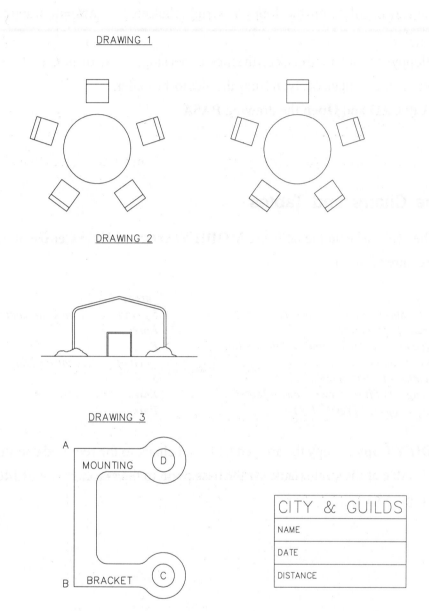

DRAWING 1

DRAWING 2

DRAWING 3

A

MOUNTING   D

BRACKET   C

B

CITY & GUILDS

NAME

DATE

DISTANCE

Pre-prepared files

To complete this assignment the pre-prepared drawings **PA5A**, **PA5B** and **PA5C** are needed.
Your tutor will provide you with the location of these files.

You may also download the files from the publisher's website at www.payne-gallway.co.uk.

3.2

Copying the Drawing Files

■ To copy the drawing files from the floppy disk, right click on the **Start** button and click on **Explore**.

■ Click the floppy drive icon and click on the files, either singly, or with the **CTRL** key held down, select them simultaneously and drag the files to the folder.

■ Execute AutoCAD and **Open** the drawing **PA5A**.

3.3

Creating the Chairs and Tables

■ To copy the chairs around the table use **MODIFY/Array** with the **Centre** of the array being the centre of the table

```
Command:                                       _array
Select objects: Specify opposite corner:       5 found      ( pick the chair)
Select objects:                                Enter
Enter the type of array [Rectangular/Polar] <R>:   P
Specify center point of array:                 _cen of      (centre of the circle)
Enter the number of items in the array:        5
Specify the angle to fill (+=ccw, -=cw) <360>: Enter
Rotate arrayed objects? [Yes/No] <Y>:          Enter
```

■ Use **MODIFY/Copy** to copy the arrayed table and chairs to the required coordinates using the **Centre** of the circle (table) as the base point to the second point of **140, 23** as shown in Figure 5.1.

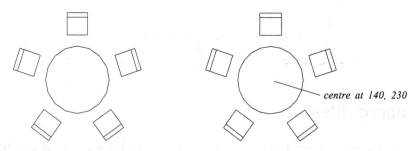

centre at 140, 230

Figure 5.1 *The completed table and chairs*

3.4

Editing the Building

- Use **MODIFY/Offset** to copy the outline of the door frame by a distance of **1** to the outside.
- Use **MODIFY/Fillet** to fillet the wall and roof junctions with a radius of **5**.
- Follow this with **MODIFY/Offset** and a distance of **2** as shown in Figure 5.2.
- Use **MODIFY/Trim** to break the building outline with the shrubbery as the cutting edges.
- Use **MODIFY/Move** to reposition the drawing to the required co-ords using the **Endpoint** as shown in Figure 5.2.

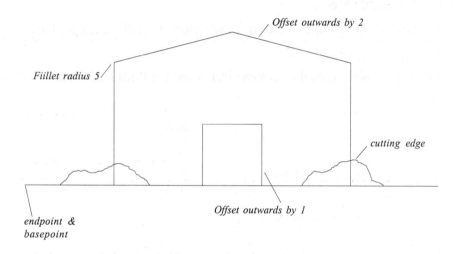

Figure 5.2 *The incomplete building drawing*

3.5

Scaling the Building

- Use **MODIFY/Scale** to reduce the size of the drawing to **0.5** using the coordinates **25, 140** as the **base point** as shown in Figure 5.2.

3.6

Editing the Mounting Bracket

The only problem with this exercise is that you will find that the completed drawing conflicts with the 'Drawing 3' after it is moved to its new coordinate position. Consult your tutor on this before you start.

- Before editing the bracket, type the variable **MIRRTEXT** at the command line and set it to **0** (zero) so that the text will not be reversed when we mirror the drawing.

- Use **MODIFY/Mirror** to mirror the drawing, with the mirror lines at the **ENDpoint** of points A and B.
- Answer **Yes** to delete old objects.

- Use **MODIFY/Break** to break the circles in an anticlockwise direction with the **First** and **Second** points as shown in Figure 5.3.
- **MODIFY/ Fillet** the junctions of the broken circles and the lines with a radius of **5** as required.

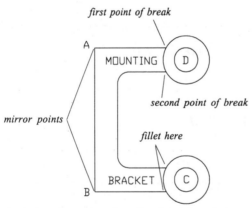

Figure 5.3 *The Bracket drawing showing the break points*

3.7

Moving the Bracket

- **MODIFY/Move** the bracket using the base point at the **ENDpoint** of line B to the required co-ordinates of **40, 40**.

3.8

Determining the Distance

■ To ensure that the distance is measured to four decimal places use **FORMAT/Units** and the **Drawing Units** dialogue box will appear as shown in Figure 5.4.

■ Set the **Length Precision** to **4** places of decimal.

■ Use **TOOLS/Inquiry/Distance** to find the distance from the **END**point of line **A** to the **Centre** circle **C** (68.0074) and enter this into the box as required.

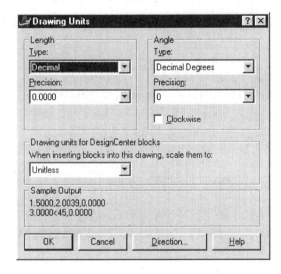

Figure 5.4 *The Units Control dialogue box with precision set to four decimal places*

3.9

Entering Your Details

■ Enter your name and the date in the box provided.

3.10

Saving the Finished Drawing

■ To save the drawing use **FILE/Save As** and save the completed project to your floppy disk or to a folder with the name **PA5AE**.

If you use **FILE/Save** AutoCAD will perform a quick save and overwrite the original unedited drawing.

4351-01-PA5B

Target Drawing - Part Two

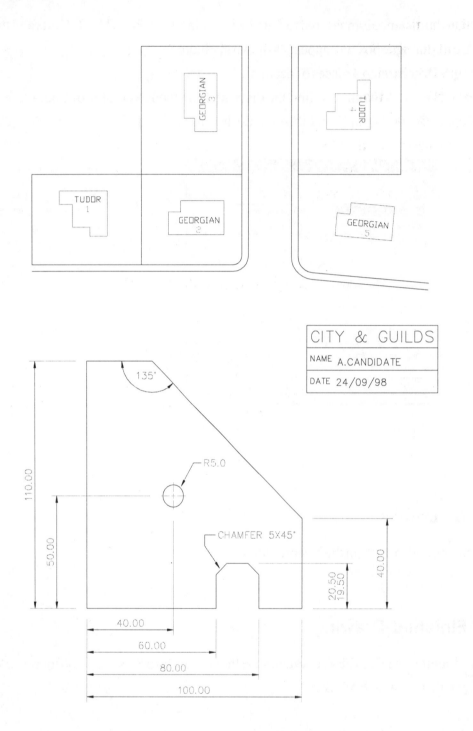

3.11

Inserting the Drawing PA5B

- Firstly, **Open** the drawing **PA5C**.

- Your tutor will provide you with the location of the pre-prepared drawing **PA5B** which you are required to place in the drawing at coordinates **20, 200**.

- Use **INSERT/Block** and click on **Browse** to locate the file and the name will appear as shown in Figure 5.5.

- Check off the '**Specify parameters on Screen**' button and enter the x,y coordinates of **20, 200** ensuring that the scale factor and rotation angle are **1** and **0** respectively. (You can also specify the coordinate position on the command line instead of specifying them here).

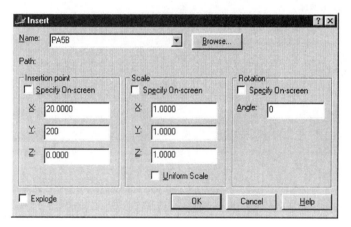

Figure 5.5 *The Insert dialogue box*

3.12

Creating a User Coordinate System

The Model Space UCS icon can be repositioned in the drawing to create a user-coordinate system with an origin specified by the user. This position then becomes the origin of the drawing.

We are required to move the origin of the drawing to the end of the lower left hand line of drawing **PA5B**.

- Use **TOOLS/Move UCS** and pick the **Endpoint** of the line as required. At this stage the icon may not physically move to the end of the line.

- Use **VIEW/Display/UCS Icon/Origin** to display the icon at its new position.

- To ensure that the **UCS** icon is visible at this position use **VIEW/Display/UCS Icon/On**.

- To save the new **UCS** position with the name **HOUSES**, type **UCS** at the command line and **Save** the name.

3.13

Creating the Blocks

This part of the exercise requires us to create two blocks with attribute data attached. The mode of the attribute data varies, enabling the user to alter the data contents of the block at insertion time and with prompts appearing, originated by the user.

The method is to draw the outline of the required drawing, create the attribute data for each incidence of an attribute (in this case we will have to define an attribute three times for each block) and lastly, save the drawing and attribute data as a block.

- Make the **Current** layer **Walls**.
- Use **DRAW/Line** (or polyline) to draw the outline of the shape **'TUDOR'** in any area of the PA5C drawing.
- Make the **Current** layer **Style**.
- Use **DRAW/Block/Define Attributes** and the **Attribute Definition** dialogue box appears as shown in Figure 5.6.
- Type in the tag **'T1'**,
- Type in the name **'TUDOR'** (which is constant and visible) and the required text style and height.
- Use **Pick Point** to choose the position for the tag inside the boundary of the Tudor drawing as shown in Figure 5.6. The name **'TUDOR'** will not appear until the drawing becomes a block.

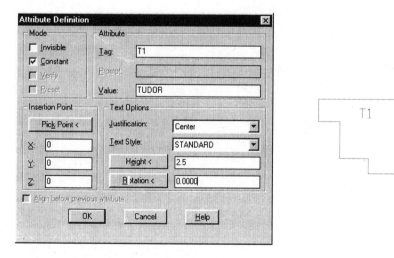

Figure 5.6 *The Attribute Definition dialogue box and the Tudor drawing with first constant attribute*

- Make the **Current** layer **Number**.

- Use **DRAW/Block/Define Attributes** to create the second attribute. The **Attribute Definition** dialogue box appears as shown in Figure 5.7 but this time the attribute mode is variable i.e. every time you insert the block into the drawing, the user will be prompted to enter a number for the plot (in this case **1** and **4**). You will see from the dialogue box in Figure 5.7 that as the attribute can vary in its value, a meaningful prompt to the user needs to be included.

- Click on the '**Align below previous attribute button**' and the tag is placed as shown in Figure 5.7.

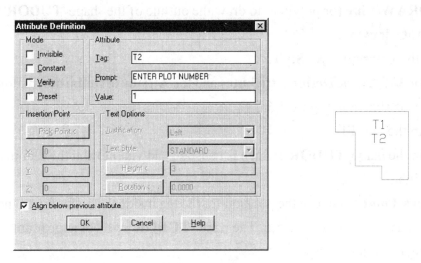

Figure 5.7 *The Attribute Definition dialogue box with the second variable attribute positioned*

- Make the **Current** layer **Cost**.
- Use **DRAW/Block/Define Attributes** once more to create the third attribute. The **Attribute Definition** dialogue box appears as shown in Figure 5.8 and again the attribute mode is variable but this time it is invisible – i.e. it does not automatically appear in the block as data unless prompted with the **ATTDISP/ON** command. You will see again from the dialogue box in Figure 5.8 that as the attribute can vary in its value, a meaningful prompt to the user needs to be included.
- Click on the **'Align below previous attribute button'** and the tag is placed as shown in Figure 5.8.

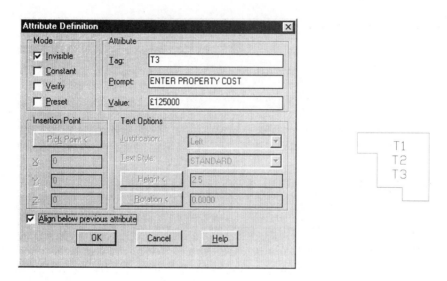

Figure 5.8 *The Attribute Definition dialogue box with the third variable attribute positioned*

To Create a Block of the Drawing

- Make the **Current** layer **0**.

- To create a block of the drawing to include its attributes, use **DRAW/Block/Make** and the **Block Definition** dialogue box will appear as shown in Figure 5.9.

- Enter the name **TUDOR**, and click on **Pick point** to choose the **INTERsection** of the corner as its required insertion base point.

- Lastly, **Select Objects** and select the drawing outline and attribute tags. The block will stay on screen as separate objects if **Retain Objects** is checked.

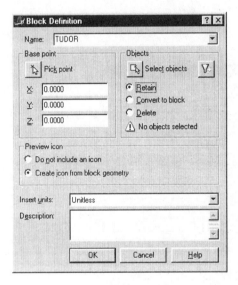

Figure 5.9 *The Block Definition dialogue box with the Tudor block name*

- Make the **Current** layer **Walls**.

- Use **DRAW/Line** to draw the outline of the shape **'GEORGIAN'** in any area of the PA5C drawing. Repeat the sequence exactly as you did for the making of the **TUDOR** block including the layer changes.

3.14

Creating the Blocks as Separate Drawings

Creating a block in a drawing makes that block available to that drawing only. To be able to insert the block in any other drawing we can create the block as a separate drawing using the **WBLOCK** command (which stands for '**Write Block**').

■ Type **WBLOCK** at the command line and the **Write Block** dialogue box will appear as shown in Figure 5.10.

■ Click on **Block** as the **Source** and scroll through the pull-down list and choose the **TUDOR** block.

■ Enter the file name **TUDOR** under **Destination/ Filename** and choose the file location in this portion also.

■ Click on **OK**.

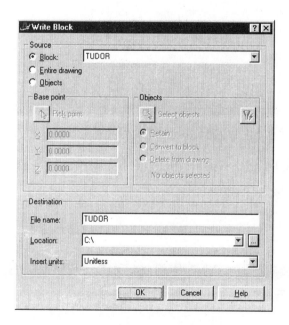

Figure 5.10 *The Write Block dialogue box*

■ Repeat the operation for the '**GEORGIAN**' Wblock.

3.15

Completing the Housing Estate

To insert the **TUDOR** block at $^1/_3$ and $^1/_4$ from the plot corner number 1, we can use **INQUIRY/ID point** to locate the insertion point of the Tudor block relative to the top left of the plot.

■ Make layer **0** the **Current** layer.

■ Use **INQUIRY/ID Point** at the **Intersection** as shown in Figure 5.11.

> *Command:*   **id**   *(pick the point as shown in Figure 5.11)*
> *Specify point: _int of X = 20.0000*   *Y = 243.0000*   *Z = 0.0000*

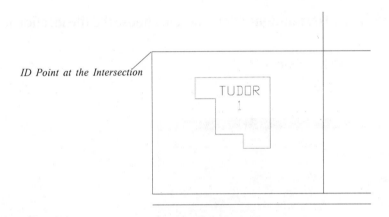

Figure 5.11   *The Tudor block in its final position*

■ Use **INSERT/Block** and the **Insert** dialogue box will appear as shown in Figure 5.12.

■ Click on **TUDOR** in the **Name** pull-down.

■ Click on **OK**.

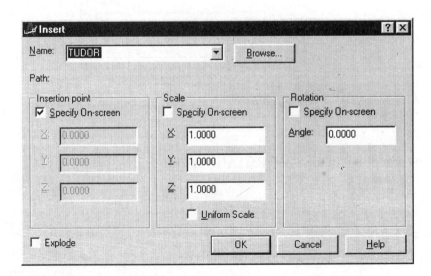

Figure 5.12   *The Insert dialogue box*

■ The dialogue will disappear and the command line prompts for an insertion point

Command: _*insert* (activates the **Insert** dialogue box as shown in Figure 5.11)*
Specify insertion point or [Scale/X/Y/Z/Rotate/PScale/PX/PY/PZ/PRotate]: @12.5,-13.3333

■ This is followed immediately by the appearance of the **Enter Attributes** dialogue box as shown in Figure 5.13.

■ Ensure that the variable **Attdia** is set to **1** for the dialogue box to appear.

You will see the prompts for the variable attributes and the default values appearing here.

■ In this instance there is no change so click on **OK** and the block is placed in its correct position.

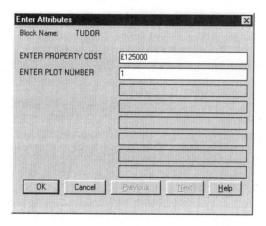

Figure 5.13 The Enter Attributes dialogue box

 ■ Repeat the operation for the next insertion of the **TUDOR** block with the insertion point at coordinates **150, 85** and rotation angle of **270°**(or **-90°**) entered in the **Insert** dialogue box.

■ Change the plot number in the **Attribute Definition** dialogue box to **4**.

  ■ To insert the **GEORGIAN** block at ¹/₃ and ¹/₄ from the plot corner we can use **ID Point** again to locate the insertion point of the blocks at **Relative** distances to the **INTERsections** of the plots as shown in Figure 5.14.

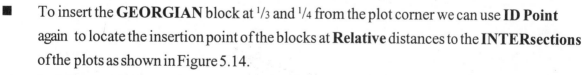 ■ In the **Insert** dialogue box place checks in the **Insertion Point - Specify On-screen and Rotation** boxes so that we can enter the **Relative** distances to the **ID** point on the commmand line as shown in Figure 5.14.

■ Change the plot numbers in the **Enter Attributes** dialogue box.

■ To insert plot number 5 aligned with the road frontage insert it at coordinates **140, 16** and a rotation angle of **355°** (or **-5°**).

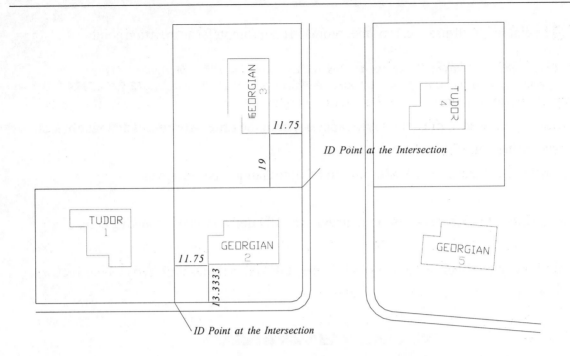

Figure 5.14 *The positions of the blocks relative to the Intersections of the plots*

3.16

Creating a Dimension Style

In preparation for dimensioning we are required to create an associative (grouped objects) dimension style called **CGTEST** on its own layer. This is done through the **DIMENSION/Style** command where the style attributes are applied and saved.

You may find it more convenient to complete the dimensions in the order shown in Figure 5.20.

- Use **FORMAT/DimensionStyle** to activate the **Dimension Style Manager** dialogue box.

- Click on the **New** button and the **Create New Dimension Style** dialogue box will overlay the first.

- Type in the name **CGTEST** and click the **Continue** button as shown in Figure 5.15.

- The **New Dimension Style** dialogue box will appear with the **Lines and Arrows** tab active.

- Change the values to those described in Objective 3.18. Some are highlighted with a black rectangle as shown in Figure 5.16.

- Repeat the operation for **Text** and **Tolerances** as shown in Figures 5.17 and 5.18 respectively.

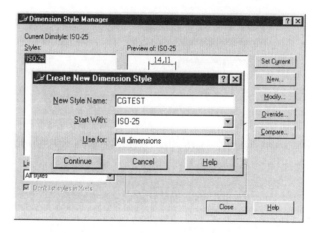

Figure 5.15 *The Dimension Style Manager dialogue box with the CGTEST style created*

- In the **Primary Units** tab dialogue box click on **Precision** and change the values so that the linear precision is to two decimal places as shown in Figure 5.19.

- Click on **OK** and the **Dimension Style Manager** dialogue box reappears.

- Click on the style name **CGTEST**, **Set Current** and **Close**.

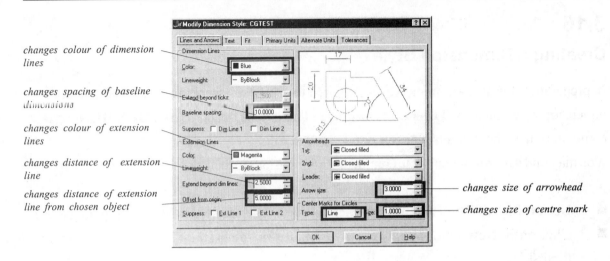

changes colour of dimension lines

changes spacing of baseline dimensions

changes colour of extension lines

changes distance of extension line

changes distance of extension line from chosen object

changes size of arrowhead

changes size of centre mark

Figure 5.16 *The Lines and Arrows tab dialogue box with the required changes highlighted*

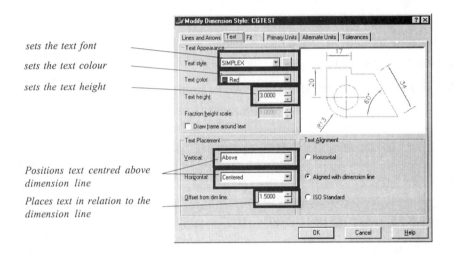

sets the text font

sets the text colour

sets the text height

Positions text centred above dimension line

Places text in relation to the dimension line

Figure 5.17 *The Text tab dialogue box with the required changes highlighted*

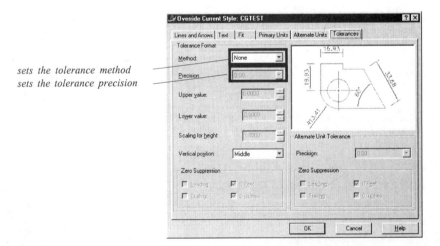

sets the tolerance method
sets the tolerance precision

Figure 5.18 *The Tolerances tab dialogue box with the required changes highlighted*

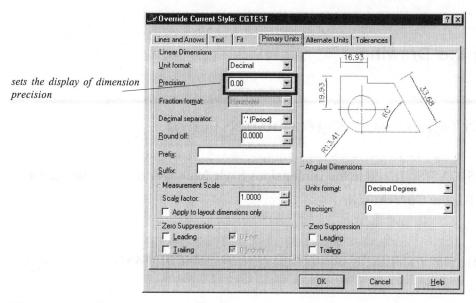

sets the display of dimension precision

Figure 5.19 *The Primary Units dialogue box with changes highlighted*

You can now dimension the drawing by following the instructions in objective 3.18.

3.17

Creating a New Layer

■ Use **FORMAT/Layer** to create a new layer.

■ Click on **New** and the word **Layer1** will appear in the list.

■ Overtype the word **Layer1** with **CGDIMENS**.

3.18
Dimensioning the Drawing

a)

- Use **FORMAT/Layers** to make the layer **CGDIMENS Current**.
- Click on **OK**.

- Use **DIMENSIONS/Style** and in the **Dimensions Style Manager** dialogue box ensure that **CGTEST** is the **Current** style.

b)

To ensure that all dimensions are associative, the system variable **DIMASO**, which defaults to **On**, needs to remain in that state.

- Type **DIMASO** at the command line and ensure that it is **On**.

c)

To prevent dimensions overlapping the Dimension line spacing needs to be set to a suitable figure. We have set our spacing to 10 as shown in the **Lines and Arrows** tab dialogue box, Figure 5.16.

d)

To ensure that a degree symbol is inserted with the leader text we can use the text control code **%%d** which places a degree symbol after the text '45' and will be entered as **'CHAMFER 5X45%%d'**.

e)

The centre line (not mark as in the instructions) in the circle is entered with the **DIMENSION/Centre mark** command and the size of the mark is governed by the **Lines and Arrows tab** dialogue box **Centre mark for Circles** option with a size of **1** which we set in Figure 5.16.

I suggest that you tackle the dimensioning in the numbered order as shown in Figure 5.20 as it will be quicker and less frustrating until you become experienced with interchanging dimensioning values.

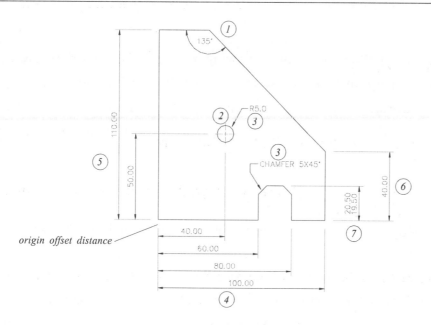

Figure 5.20 *The completed PA5CE drawing*

<u>*1*</u>

- Use **FORMAT/Dimension Style** and click on **Override**.
- To enter the angular value, in the **Text** tab dialogue box change the **Vertical Text Placement** to **JIS**.
- Click the **Horizontal Text alignment** button to **On**.
- Set **Offset from dim line** to **3**.
- **OK** and **Close** through the dialogue boxes.
- Use **DIMENSION/Angular** and place the angle as required.

<u>*2*</u>

- Use **DIMENSION/Center Mark** to place the **Centre Mark** and **Centre Line** in the circle.

<u>*3*</u>

- Use **FORMAT/Dimension Style** and click on **Override** in the **Dimension Style Manager** dialogue box.
- In the **Text** tab dialogue box change the **Vertical Text Placement** to **Centred** which will place the leader text central to the leader line.
- Use **DIMENSION/Leader** and draw the leader and text **'R5.0'**.
- Repeat the operation for the second leader and enter the text **'CHAMFER 5x45%%d'** which will convert the control code to a degree symbol as described in 3.18d above.

_4/5_

The 'stacked' dimensions at the bottom and left of the drawing are achieved through the **Lines and Arrows** tab dialogue box which we have already set to a value of **10** through **Baseline spacing**. In addition, the distance between the extension line as shown in Figure 5.20 and the endpoint of the measured object is set through the **Lines and Arrows** tab dialogue box with **Offset from Origin** which we have already set to 5.

- Use **FORMAT/Dimension Style** and click on **Override**.
- In the **Text** tab change the **Vertical Text Placement** to **Above** which will place the text above the leader line.
- Change **Text Alignment** to **Aligned with dimension line**.
- To draw the distance of **40.00** under the drawing use **DIMENSION/Linear** and choose the left hand **END**point of the line and the **END**point of the **Center Mark**. The endpoint of the centre mark is chosen to maintain the origin offset distance.
- Use **DIMENSION/Baseline** and select the second dimension line origin as shown in Figure 5.20.
- Repeat the operation for the vertical left hand dimensions.

_6_

- Use **DIMENSION/Linear** and press **Enter**, select the line (not the endpoints) and place the dimension as required.

_7_

- Use **FORMAT/Dimension Style** and click on **Override**.
- To place the dimension text with tolerance limits, in the **Tolerances** tab dialogue box set the **Tolerance Format Method** to **Limits** and enter the **Upper** and **Lower** values to 0.5.
- Use **DIMENSION/Linear** to place the dimension.

3.19
Saving the View

- To save the view of the titlebox use **VIEW/Zoom/Window** and place a zoom window around the box ensuring that only the box is visible on screen.
- At the command line type **VIEW** and the **View** dialogue box will appear.
- Click on **New** and the **New View** dialogue box will overlay the previous.
- Type **Title** as the **View Name**.
- Click on **OK** in both dialogue boxes.

3.20
Editing the Titlebox Attributes

You are required to edit the attributes in the titlebox to provide your own name and date.

- Use **MODIFY/Attribute/Single** and after clicking on the title box the **Edit Attributes** dialogue box will appear as shown in figure 5.21.
- Overwrite the current details with your own.

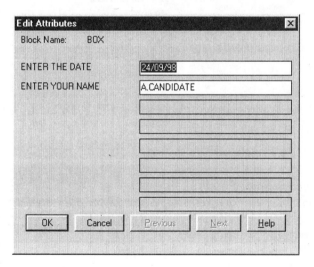

Figure 5.21 *The Edit Attributes dialogue box*

3.21

Changing the Name and Removing unused Blocks

To change the name of the block called **Box** to **Box2**

■ Use **FORMAT/Rename** and the **Rename** dialogue box appears as shown in Figure 5.22.

■ Select **Blocks** and then the **Item** called **BOX**.

■ Enter **BOX2** in the **Rename** box and click on **OK**.

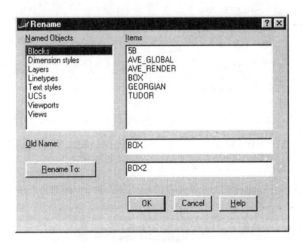

Figure 5.22 *The Rename Objects dialogue box*

■ To remove unused blocks from the drawing we can use **FILE/Drawing Utilities/Purge/ Blocks** and the command line will prompt

Command: _purge
Enter type of unused objects to purge
[Blocks/Dimstyles/LAyers/LTypes/Plotstyles/SHapes/textSTyles/Mlinestyles/All]:
_b Enter name(s) to purge <*>:　　　　　　**TITLEBOX**
Verify each name to be purged? [Yes/No] <Y>:　　**Enter**
Purge block "TITLEBOX"? <N>　　　　　　　**Y**

3.22

Saving the Drawing

■ To save the drawing use **FILE/Save As** and save the completed project to your selected folder or directory.

If you use **File/Save** AutoCAD will perform a quick save to the original PA5C drawing.

3.23

Copying the Completed Drawing Files

■ To copy the drawing files from your folder, right click on the **Start** button and click on **Explore**.

■ Locate the folder and files.

■ Click on the files, either singly, or with the **CTRL** key held down, select them simultaneously and drag the files to the floppy drive icon.

4351-01-PA6

Target Drawing - Part 1- PA6A

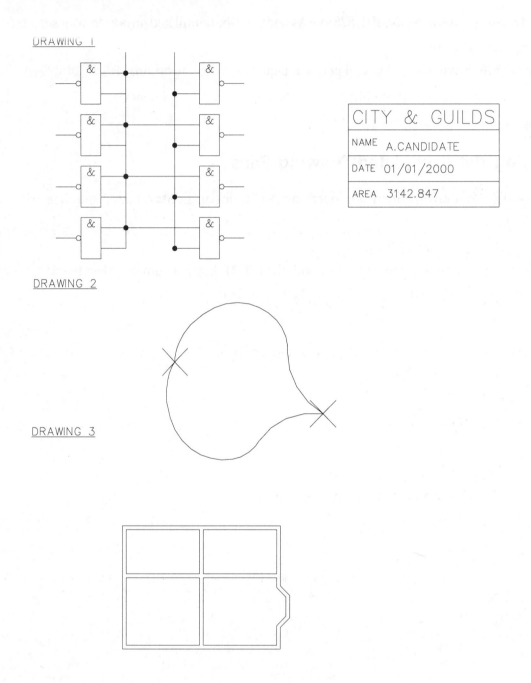

Pre-prepared files

To complete this assignment the pre-prepared drawings **PA6A**, **PA6B** and **PA6C** are needed.
Your tutor will provide you with the location of these files.

 You may also download the files from the publisher's website at www.payne-gallway.co.uk.

3.2

Copying the Drawing Files

- To copy the drawing files from the floppy disk, right click on the **Start** button and click on **Explore**.

- Click the floppy drive icon and click on the files, either singly, or with the **CTRL** key held down, select them simultaneously and drag the files to the folder.

- Execute AutoCAD and **Open** the drawing **PA6A**.

3.3

Creating the Electrical Components

Firstly we will copy the single component upwards using the Array command, followed by mirroring to provide the identical copy **20** units to the left.

To copy the single component

- Use **MODIFY/Array/Rectangular** to copy with **4 rows, 1 column** and a **distance** of **20** between the rows as required.

- Use **DRAW/Line** to draw a line from the **ENDpoint** of the line as shown in Figure 6.1 to co-ordinates **70, 260**.

- Set **Grid** and **Snap** to **10** and turn **On**.

- Use **MODIFY/ Mirror** to mirror the components using the snap and grid as the upper and lower mirror points **10** units to the left of the drawing as shown in Figure 6.1.

- Answer **NO** to deleting old objects.

- Use **DRAW/Donut** to add **Donuts** in the required positions, snapping to the **INTersections** of the lines.

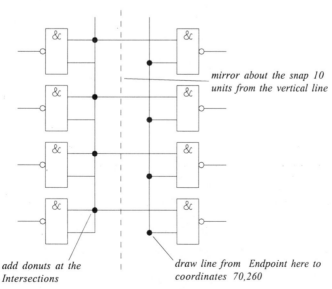

mirror about the snap 10 units from the vertical line

add donuts at the Intersections

draw line from Endpoint here to coordinates 70,260

Figure 6.1 *The completed electrical drawing*

3.4

Placing a Point Entity

■ Change the point mode with **FORMAT/Point Style** and the **Point Style** dialogue box will appear as shown in Figure 6.2.

■ Click on the cross as shown and click on **OK**.

The Point command will now generate a cross on the drawing.

■ Turn **Snap Off**.

■ Use **DRAW/Point** and place a point at the end of the polyline as required and at coordinates **130, 120**.

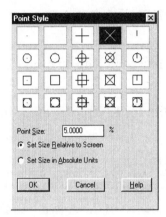

Figure 6.2 The Point Style dialogue box

3.5/3.6

Editing and Smoothing the Polyline

The requirement is to move the right hand endpoint of the polyline to the point at coordinates **130, 120**. The command Polyedit or **PEDIT** is used to edit the vertices of the polyline by moving to the end of the vertices until the vertex to be moved is reached.

■ At the command line type **PEDIT**

Command: **pedit**
Select polyline: **pick** *the cam profile polyline*
Enter an option [Close/Join/Width/Edit vertex/Fit/Spline/Decurve/Ltype gen/Undo]:e (for
edit vertex)
Enter a vertex editing option
*[Next/Previous/Break/Insert/Move/Regen/Straighten/Tangent/Width/eXit] <N>:***Enter**
(press Enter until the point marker moves to the right hand endpoint of the polyline)

Enter a vertex editing option
[Next/Previous/Break/Insert/Move/Regen/Straighten/Tangent/Width/eXit] <N>: **m** *(for move)*
Specify new location for marked vertex: **_nod of** *(pick the point at coordinates 130, 120)*
Enter a vertex editing option
[Next/Previous/Break/Insert/Move/Regen/Straighten/Tangent/Width/eXit] <N>: **x** *(exit the*
routine)
Enter an option [Close/Join/Width/Edit vertex/Fit/Spline/Decurve/Ltype gen/Undo]: **f** *(for*
Fit curve)
*Enter an option [Close/Join/Width/Edit vertex/Fit/Spline/Decurve/Ltype gen/Undo]:***x** *(exit the*
routine)

■ Use **MODIFY/Mirror** to make an identical image of the shape using the **NODE** of the points at each end of the shape as shown in Figure 6.3, (or the **ENDpoints**) as the first and second mirror positions.

■ Answer **No** to deleting old objects.

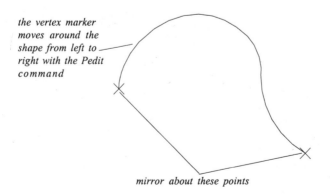

the vertex marker moves around the shape from left to right with the Pedit command

mirror about these points

Figure 6.3 *The partly finished cam profile*

3.7

Editing the Building Drawing

The single line building drawing is required have lines added to represent wall widths.

- Use **MODIFY/Offset** to create the walls of the outline of the building.

- Offset by **2** units outside and the interior line above and to the right also by **2**.

- Use **MODIFY/Trim** with a crossing window to erase the centre crossing lines as shown in Figure 6.4 and pick the inner lines to remove.

- Use **MODIFY/Break** to erase the junctions of the walls as shown in Figure 6.4.

After editing the building it is worth noting that the original drawing has a right hand room width of **50** units and after editing (Offsetting) the room is **48** units wide. The required drawing has a right hand room width of **40** units but makes no mention of changing this in the instructions. I have assumed that this omission is not intentional.

- To change the room width use **MODIFY/Stretch**

Command:	***stretch***
Select objects to stretch by crossing-window or crossing-polygon...	
Select objects: Other corner: 2 found	***(place a crossing window around the whole of the right hand side of the building)***
Select objects	***Enter***
Base point or displacement:	***_endp of*** *(pick the top right hand corner of the building)*
Second point of displacement:	***@-8,0*** *(relative coordinates - don't forget the minus)*

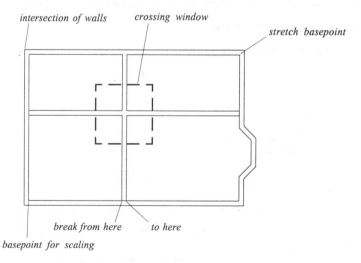

Figure 6.4 *The building before scaling*

3.8

Scaling the Building Drawing

■ Use **MODIFY/Scale** to re-size the finished drawing using the base point of **50,30** as shown in Figure 6.4 and to **0.75** of its size.

3.9

Determining the Area of the Building

■ Use **FORMAT/Units** and in the **Drawing Units** dialogue box set the **Length Precision** to 3 decimal places.

■ Use **TOOLS/Inquiry/Area** to determine the total area of the building (3142.847) using the **INTersection** of the wall ends as shown in Figure 6.4.

You may find it easier to set a running Object Snap with **TOOLS/Drafting Settings/Object snap** tab.

■ The **Drafting Settings** dialogue box will appear as shown in Figure 6.5.

■ Set the snap to **Intersection** or **Endpoint**.

■ Remember to **Clear All** when the area calculation is completed.

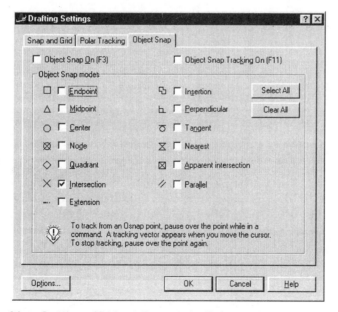

Figure 6.5 The Drafting Settings/Object Snap tab dialogue box

3.10
Entering Your Details

■ Enter your name and the date in the box provided using **DRAW/Text/Single Line Text**.

3.11
Saving the Drawing

 ■ To save the drawing use **FILE/Save As** and save the completed project to your floppy disk or to a folder with the name PA6AE.

If you use **FILE/Save** AutoCAD will perform a quick save and overwrite the original unedited drawing.

4351-01-PA6B

Target Drawing - Part Two - PA6B

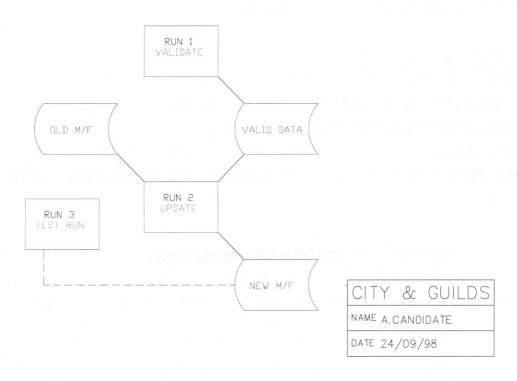

RUN 1
VALIDATE

OLD M/F

VALID DATA

RUN 2
UPDATE

RUN 3
TEST RUN

NEW M/F

CITY & GUILDS

NAME A.CANDIDATE

DATE 24/09/98

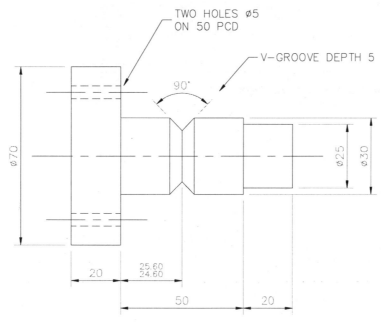

TWO HOLES ⌀5
ON 50 PCD

V-GROOVE DEPTH 5

90°

⌀70

⌀25

⌀30

20

25.60
24.60

50

20

3.12
Inserting the Drawing PA6B

Your tutor will provide you with the location of the pre-prepared drawing PA6B which you are required to place in the drawing at coordinates 105, 184.

- Firstly, **Open** the drawing **PA6C**.
- Use **INSERT/Block** and click on **Browse** to locate the file **PA6B** and the name will appear as shown in Figure 6.6.
- Remove the check in the '**Specify parameters on Screen**' button and enter the x,y coordinates of **105, 184** ensuring that the scale factor and rotation angle are **1** and **0** respectively. (You can also specify the coordinate position on the command line instead of specifying them here).

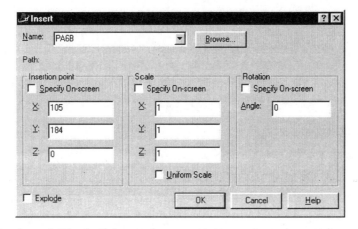

Figure 6.6 *The Insert Block dialogue box*

3.13/3.14
Creating the Blocks and Producing the Flowchart

This part of the exercise requires us to create two blocks with attribute data attached. The mode of the attribute data varies, enabling the user to alter the data contents of the block at insertion time and with prompts appearing, originated by the user.

The method is to draw the outline of the required drawing, create the attribute data for each incidence of an attribute (in this case we will have to define an attribute three times for the block '**PROCESS**' and two for '**FILE**') and lastly, save the drawing and attribute data as a block.

- Make the **Current** layer **Outline**.
- Use **DRAW/Line** (or polyline) to draw the outline of the shape '**PROCESS**' in any area of the PA6C drawing.

- Make the **Current** layer **Data**.
- Use **DRAW/Block/Define Attributes** and the **Attribute Definition** dialogue box appears as shown in Figure 6.7.
- Type in the tag '**T1**', the prompt '**ENTER DATA**' (i.e. every time you insert the block into the drawing, the user will be prompted to enter data for the flowchart block – in this case **Run 1** or **Run 2**) and the default value '**RUN 1**'.
- Enter the required text style and height.
- Use **Pick Point** to choose the position for the tag inside the boundary of the **PROCESS** drawing as shown in Figure 6.7.

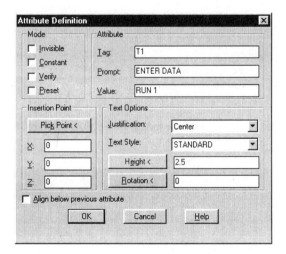

Figure 6.7 *The Attribute Definition dialogue box and the File drawing with first variable attribute*

■ Make the **Current** layer **Type**.

■ Use **DRAW/Block/Define Attributes** again to create the second attribute. The **Attribute Definition** dialogue box appears as shown in Figure 6.8 and again the attribute mode is variable. You will see from the dialogue box in Figure 6.8 that as the attribute can vary in its value, a meaningful prompt to the user needs to be included.

■ Click on the **'Align below previous attribute button'** and the tag is placed as shown in Figure 6.8.

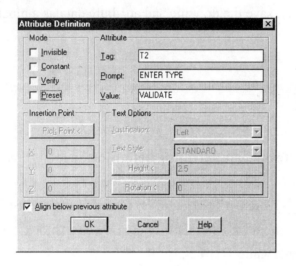

Figure 6.8 *The Attribute Definition dialogue box with the second variable attribute positioned*

- Make the **Current** layer **Code**.
- Use **DRAW/Block/Define Attributes** once more to create the third attribute. The **Attribute Definition** dialogue box appears as shown in Figure 6.9 and again the attribute mode is variable but this time it is invisible i.e. it does not automatically appear in the block as data unless prompted with the **ATTDISP/ON** command. You will see again from the dialogue box in Figure 6.9 that as the attribute can vary in its value, a meaningful prompt to the user needs to be included.

- Click on the **'Align below previous attribute button'** and the tag is placed as shown in Figure 6.9.

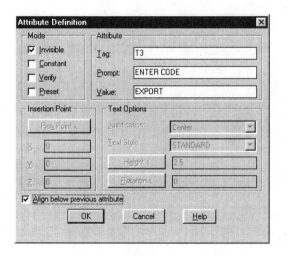

Figure 6.9 *The Attribute Definition dialgue box with the third variable attribute positioned*

To Create a Block of the Drawing

- Make the **Current** layer **0**.

- To create a block of the drawing to include its attributes, use **DRAW/Block/Make** and the **Block Definition** dialogue box will appear as shown in Figure 6.10.

- Enter the **Name PROCESS**, and click on **Select point** to choose the **INTERsection** of the corner as its insertion base point.

- Lastly, **Select Objects** and select the outline and attribute tags. The block will stay on screen as separate objects if **Retain Objects** is checked.

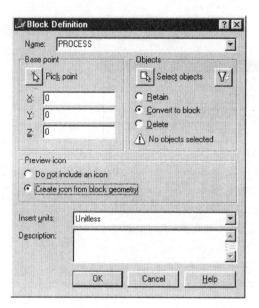

Figure 6.10   *The Block Definition dialogue box*

- Make the **Current** layer **Outline**.

- Use **DRAW/Line** to draw the outline of the shape **'FILE'** in any area of the PA6C drawing.

- Repeat the sequence exactly as you did for the making of the **PROCESS** block including the layer changes.

3.15

Creating the Blocks as Separate Drawings

Creating a block in a drawing makes that block available to that drawing only. To be able to insert the block in any other drawing we can create the block as a separate drawing using the **WBLOCK** command (which stands for 'Write Block').

- Type **WBLOCK** at the command line and the **Write Block** dialogue box will appear as shown in Figure 6.11.

- Click on **Block** as the **Source** and scroll through the pull-down list and choose the **PROCESS** block.

- Enter the file name **PROCESS** under **Destination/ Filename** and choose the **Destination Location** in this portion also.

- Click on **OK**.

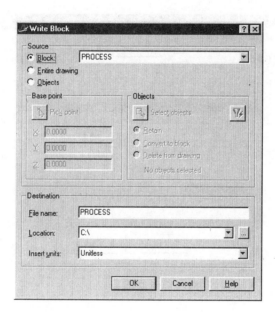

Figure 6.11   *The Write Block dialogue box*

- Repeat the operation for the **'FILE'** Wblock.

3.16

Completing the Flowchart

We are required to insert the blocks at the **Endpoints** of the lines but, as the block insertion points do not coincide it is easier to insert the blocks near the lines and move them later.

- Make layer **0** the **Current** layer.
- Use **INSERT/Block** and the **Insert** dialogue box will appear as shown in Figure 6.12.
- Scroll through the **Name** pull-down and click on **FILE.**
- Place a check in the **Insertion point Specify on screen** box so that we can pick an arbitrary insertion point on screen.
- Click on **OK**.

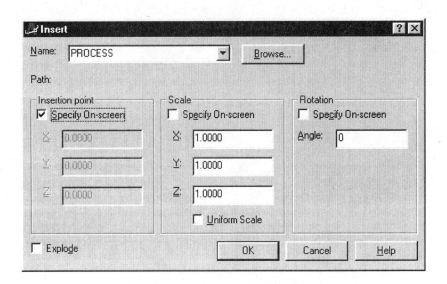

Figure 6.12 The Insert dialogue box

- After choosing an insertion point this is followed immediately by the appearance of the **Enter Attributes** dialogue box. You will see the prompts for the variable attributes and the default values appearing here.
- Change the default values as required for **Old M/F**, **New M/F** and **Valid Data**.

- After entering the attribute data use **MODIFY/ Move** to move the blocks using **Object snaps** to the ends of the lines.

- Use **INSERT/Block** to insert the **PROCESS** block and then **MODIFY/Move** to the ends of the lines.
- To draw the broken line change the linetype to the **Hidden** linestyle.

- Turn **Ortho On**.

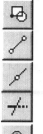

- To insert the **PROCESS** block at $^1/_3$ and $^1/_4$ from the File and Process Blocks, we can draw 2 lines, one from the **Midpoint** of the **New M/F File** block and one from the bottom **Endpoint** of the **Old M/F File** block to meet at their intersection.
- Draw them beyond their intersection and use **MODIFY/Trim** to form the right angle as shown in Figure 6.13.
- **MODIFY/Offset** the vertical line to the left by **7.5** ($^1/_4$ of 30).
- Draw a line from the bottom left corner of the **Run 2 Update** attribute **Perpendicular** to the vertical line.
- **MODIFY/Offset** this line downwards by **6.6666** ($^1/_3$ of 20).
- **MODIFY/Extend** the line to meet the offset vertical line as shown in Figure 6.13.
- Use **INSERT/Block** and the **Insert** dialogue box will appear again, as shown in Figure 6.12.
- Click on **OK** and insert the block at the **Intersection** of the two lines as shown in Figure 6.13.
- This is followed immediately by the appearance of the **Enter Attributes** dialogue box again. You will see, here, the prompts for the variable attributes and the default values appearing.
- Change the default values to **Run 3** and **Test Run**.
- Use **MODIFY/Erase** to delete the offset lines and the line drawn from **RUN 2 UPDATE**.
- **MODIFY/Break** the vertical line at the base of the the newly inserted **PROCESS** block.
- Set the linetype back to **Bylayer**.

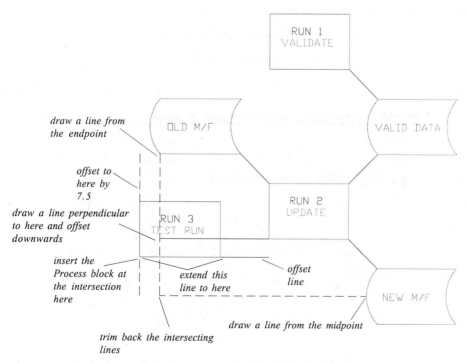

Figure 6.13 *The partly completed Flowchart diagram*

3.17

Creating a Dimension Style

In preparation for dimensioning we are required to create an associative (grouped objects) dimension style called **CGTEST** on its own layer. This is done through the **DIMENSION/Style** command where the style attributes are applied and saved.

You may find it more convenient to complete the dimensions in the order shown in figure 6.19.

■ Use **FORMAT/DimensionStyle** to activate the **Dimension Style Manager** dialogue box.

■ Click on the **New** button and the **Create New Dimension Style** dialogue box will overlay the first.

■ Type in the name **CGTEST** and click the **Continue** button as shown in Figure 6.14.

The **New Dimension Styles** dialogue box will appear with the **Lines and Arrows** tab active.

■ Change the values to those described in Objective 3.19. Some values are highlighted with a black rectangle as shown in Figure 6.15.

■ Repeat the operation for **Text** and **Tolerances** as shown in Figures 6.16 and 6.17. respectively.

■ In the **Primary Units** tab dialogue box click on **Precision** and change the values so that the linear precision is to **0** decimal places.

■ Click on **OK** and the **Dimension Style Manager** dialogue box reappears.

■ Click on the style name **CGTEST**, **Set Current** and **Close**.

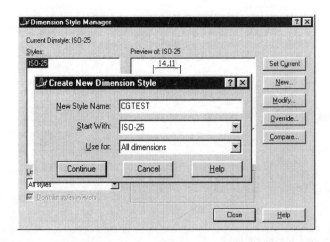

Figure 6.14 *The Dimension Style Manager dialogue box with the CGTEST style created*

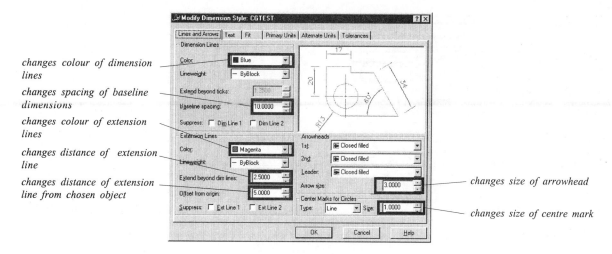

changes colour of dimension lines

changes spacing of baseline dimensions

changes colour of extension lines

changes distance of extension line

changes distance of extension line from chosen object

changes size of arrowhead

changes size of centre mark

Figure 6.15 *The Lines and Arrows tab dialogue box with the required changes highlighted*

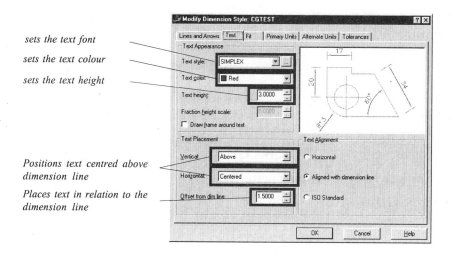

sets the text font

sets the text colour

sets the text height

Positions text centred above dimension line

Places text in relation to the dimension line

Figure 6.16 *The Text tab dialogue box with the required changes highlighted*

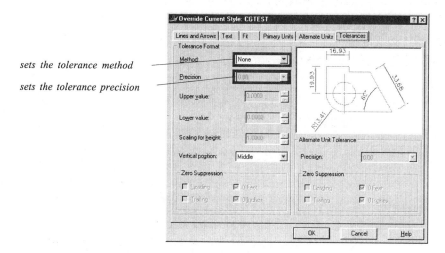

sets the tolerance method

sets the tolerance precision

Figure 6.17 *The Tolerances tab dialogue box with the required changes highlighted*

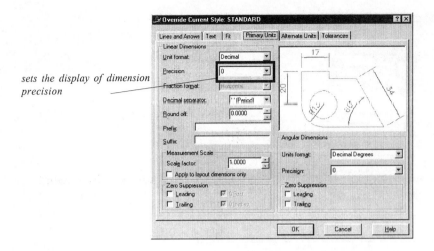

sets the display of dimension precision

Figure 6.18   *The Primary Units tab dialogue box with changes highlighted*

You can now dimension the drawing by following the instructions in objective 3.19.

3.18

Creating a New Layer

■   Activate the **Layer** dialogue box by using **FORMAT/Layer**.

■   Click on **New** and the word **Layer1** will appear in the list.

■   Simply overtype this with **CGDIMENS**.

■   Click on **OK**.

3.19
Dimensioning the Drawing

a)

- Use **FORMAT/Layer** to make the layer **CGDIMENS Current**.
- Click on **OK**.
- Use **DIMENSIONS/Style** and in the **Dimensions Style Manager** dialogue box ensure that **CGTEST** is **Set Current**.

b)

To ensure that all dimensions are associative, the system variable **DIMASO**, which defaults to **On**, needs to remain in that state.

- Type **DIMASO** at the command line and ensure that it is **On**.

c)

- To prevent dimensions overlapping the Dimension line spacing needs to be set to a suitable figure. We have set our spacing to **10** as shown in the **Lines and Arrows** tab dialogue box, Figure 6.15.

d)

To ensure that a diameter symbol is inserted on the dimension line and on the leader text
- Enter the text control code **%%c** which places a diameter symbol before the text.

e)

The upper and lower limits are set through the **Tolerances** tab dialogue box as shown in Figure 6.17 where **Tolerance Format Method** is set to **Limits**.

- The **Upper** value is set to 0.6 and the **Lower** value to 0.4.

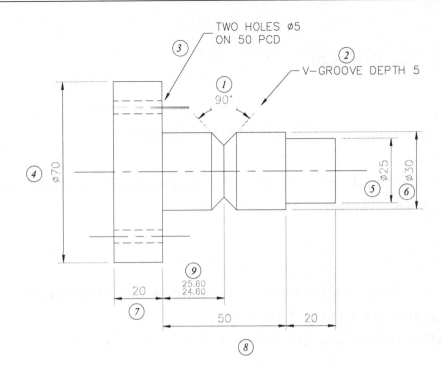

Figure 6.19 The completed PA6CE drawing

<u>*1*</u>

■ In the **Dimension Style Manager** dialogue box click on **Override**.

■ To enter the angular value, in the **Text** tab dialogue box change the **Vertical Text Placement** to **JIS**.

■ Click the **Horizontal Text alignment** button to **On**.

■ Set **Offset from dim line** to **3**.

■ Click on **OK** and **Close** through the dialogue boxes but do not save the changes.

■ Use **DIMENSION/Angular** and place the angle as required.

<u>*2/3*</u>

■ In the **Dimension Style Manager** dialogue box click on **Override**.

■ To enter the leader values, in the **Text** tab dialogue box change the **Text Placement Vertical** to **Centred** and **Text Alignment** to **Aligned with dimension line**.

■ Set **Offset from dim line** back to 1.5.

■ Draw the leader and text **'V-GROOVE DEPTH 5'**.

■ Repeat the operation for the second leader and enter the text **'TWO HOLES %%c5 ON 50 PCD'** which will convert the control code to a diameter symbol as described in 3.19d above.

■ When you end of the first line of text, press **Enter** and continue with the remainder of the line.

4

- In the **Dimension Style Manager** dialogue box click on **Override**.
- To enter the leader values, in the **Text** tab dialogue box change the **Text Placement Vertical** to **Above.**

- Use **DIMENSION/Linear** and the comand line will prompt

  Command: _dimlinear
  Specify first extension line origin or <select object>:   ***Enter***
  Select object to dimension: ***select line to dimension***
  Specify dimension line location or   ***pick*** *dimension line location*
  [Mtext/Text/Angle/Horizontal/Vertical/Rotated]:   ***T*** *(for text)*
  Enter dimension text <70>:   ***%%C70***
  Specify dimension line location or
  [Mtext/Text/Angle/Horizontal/Vertical/Rotated]:   ***pick*** *dimension line location*
  Dimension text = 70

5/6

- To draw the distance diameters of 25 and 30 use **DIMENSION/Linear** and use the same method as in *4*, above.

7/9

The 'lined-up' dimensions at the bottom of the drawing are achieved through using **DIMENSION/Linear** and **DIMENSION/Continue** with a dimension tolerance included in one dimension.

- Use **DIMENSION/Linear**, select the line and place the text.
- In the **Dimension Style Manager** dialogue box click on **Override**.
- In the **Tolerances** tab dialogue box set the **Tolerance Format Method** to **Limits**, an **Upper Value** of **0.6**, a **Lower Value** of **0.40**.
- In the **Primary Units** tab set the **Linear Dimension Precision** to **2** decimal places.
- **OK** and **Close** through the dialogue boxes.
- Using **DIMENSION/Continue**, select the endpoint of the second extension (the intersection in the lower v-groove) and the dimension will be placed adjacent to the previous.

8

- To draw the distances of **50** and **20** use **DIMENSION/Linear** and **DIMENSION/ Continue** using the same method as in *7/9* above, but in the **Tolerances** tab dialogue box set **Tolerance Format Method** to **None** and in the **Primary Units** tab set the **Linear Dimension Precision** to **0** decimal places.

3.20
Saving the View

- To save the view of the titlebox use **VIEW/Zoom/Window** and place a zoom window around the box ensuring that only the box is visible on screen.
- At the command line type **VIEW** and the **View** dialogue box will appear.
- Click on **New** and the **New View** dialogue box will overlay the previous.
- Type **Title** as the **View Name**.
- Click on **OK** in both dialogue boxes.

3.21
Editing the Titlebox Attributes

We are required to edit the attributes in the titlebox to provide your own name and date.

- Use **MODIFY/Attribute/Single** and overwrite the current details with your own as shown in Figure 6.18.

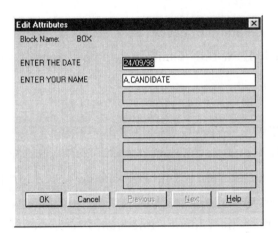

Figure 6.18 *The Edit Attributes dialogue box*

3.22

Changing the Text Style Name and Removing Unused layers

- To change the name of the text style called **Title** to **Simplex** use **FORMAT/Rename** and the **Rename** dialogue box appears as shown in Figure 6.19.

- Select **Text styles** and then the **Item** called **Title**.

- Enter **Simplex** in the **Rename** box.

- Click on **OK**.

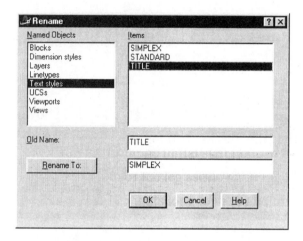

Figure 6.19   *The Rename dialogue box*

- To remove the unused layer **Walls** from the drawing we can use **FILE/Drawing Utilities/ Purge/Layers** and the command line will prompt

```
Command: _purge
Enter type of unused objects to purge
[Blocks/Dimstyles/LAyers/LTypes/Plotstyles/SHapes/textSTyles/Mlinestyles/All]:
_la Enter name(s) to purge <*>:              walls
Verify each name to be purged? [Yes/No] <Y>:   Enter
Purge layer "WALLS"? <N>                       Y
```

3.23

Saving the Drawing

■ To save the drawing use **FILE/Save As** and save the completed project to your selected folder or directory.

If you use **FILE/Save** AutoCAD will perform a quick save to the original PA5C drawing.

3.24

Copying the Completed Drawing Files

■ To copy the drawing files from your folder, right click on the **Start** button and click on **Explore**.

■ Locate the folder and files.

■ Click on the files, either singly, or with the **CTRL** key held down, select them simultaneously and drag the files to the floppy drive icon.

Target Drawing -PA7A- Part 1

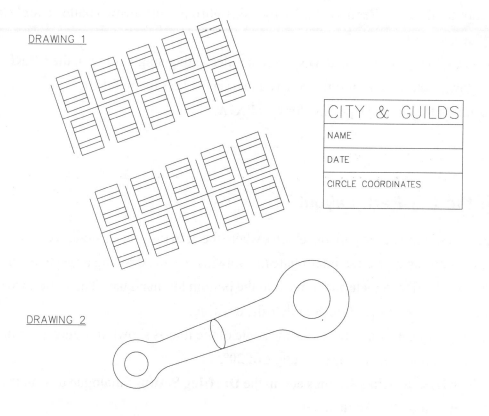

DRAWING 1

CITY & GUILDS

| NAME |
| DATE |
| CIRCLE COORDINATES |

DRAWING 2

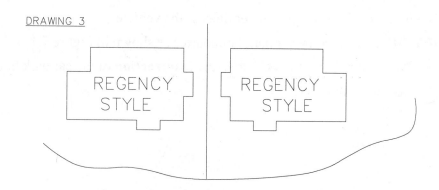

DRAWING 3

REGENCY
STYLE

REGENCY
STYLE

Pre-prepared files

To complete this assignment the pre-prepared drawings **PA7A**, **PA7B** and **PA7C** are needed.
Your tutor will provide you with the location of these files.

You may also download the files from the publisher's website at www.payne-gallway.co.uk.

3.2

Copying the Drawing Files

- To copy the drawing files from the floppy disk, right click on the **Start** button and click on **Explore**.

- Click the floppy drive icon and click on the files, either singly, or with the **CTRL** key held down, select them simultaneously and drag the files to the folder.

- Execute AutoCAD and **Open** the drawing **PA7A**.

3.3

Editing the Car Park Layout

We are required to create a car park of vehicles where the drawing is at an angle. To create the vehicle at the same angle we can interrogate the drawing, set the drawing angle to be the same value and draw the first vehicle and move it to the bottom left hand bay. Thereafter, we can use the Array and Mirror commands to complete the drawing.

- Firstly, interrogate the drawing for the angle of the line as shown in figure 7.1 with **List**. You will find that the line is at an angle of **20°**.

- Use **TOOLS/Drafting Settings** and in the **Drafting Settings** dialogue box, in the **Snap** and **Grid tab** set the **Angle** to **20°**.
  You will see the cursor change to this angle (and also the grid if you use it).

- Use **DRAW/Line** to draw the shape of the vehicle.

- Use **MODIFY/Offset** to copy the four inner lines of the vehicle.

- Use **MODIFY/Offset** to copy the car park boundaries as shown in Figure 7.1.

- Use **MODIFY/Move** to relocate the vehicle to the **Intersection** of the car park boundary temporary lines as shown in Figure 7.1.

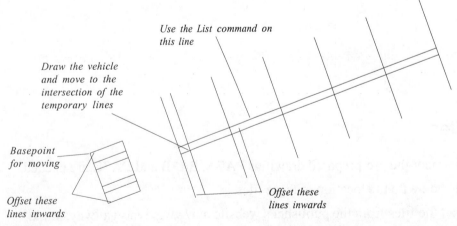

Figure 7.1 *The first vehicle drawn at the required angle and ready to move into position*

- Use **MODIFY/Erase** to delete the temporary lines.
- To complete the first double bay use **MODIFY/Array/Rectangular** to copy the vehicle with **2** rows, **5** columns and distances of **19** between the rows and **16** between columns.
- Use **DRAW/Line** to draw two temporary lines between the car park bays as shown in Figure 7.2.
- Use **MODIFY/Mirror** to copy the vehicles to the upper bays, using the **MID**points of the temporary lines as the first and second mirror points.
- Use **MODIFY/Erase** to delete the construction lines.
- Use **TOOLS/Drafting Settings** and in the **Drafting Settings** dialogue box, in the **Snap** and **Grid** tab set the **Angle** back to **0°**.

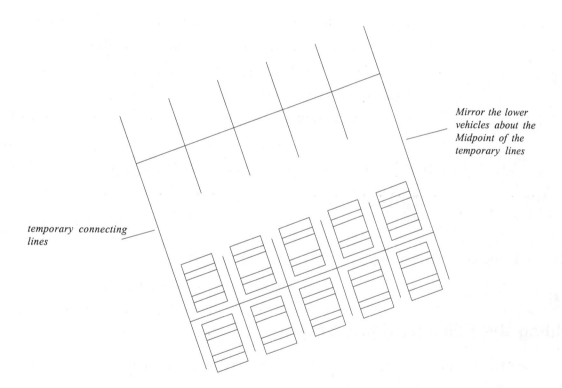

Mirror the lower vehicles about the Midpoint of the temporary lines

temporary connecting lines

Figure 7.2 *The first bays arrayed and ready to be mirrored about the temporary connecting lines*

3.4
Editing the Link Drawing

The original length of the Link drawing from circle centres is **60** units, and we are required to lengthen the drawing.

- Use **MODIFY/Stretch** to lengthen the component by placing a crossing window and stretch base point as shown in Figure 7.3 with relative coordinates **@20<0**.
- Use **MODIFY/Break** to break the circles as shown in Figure 7.3 (anti-clockwise, remember).
- **MODIFY/Fillet** the break junctions with a radius of **10**.

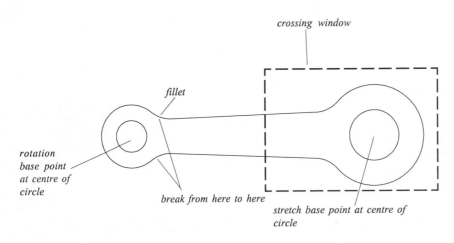

Figure 7.3 *The Link drawing after stretching, breaking and filleting*

3.5
Adding the Elliptical Cross-Section

- Use **DRAW/Ellipse** with the axis endpoints at the **MIDpoints** of the upper and lower lines and a **distance to other axis** of **2.5**.

3.6
Re-aligning the Link Drawing

- Use **MODIFY/Rotate** to turn the component through **20°** with a rotation base point at the **Centre** of the small circle as shown in Figure 7.3.

3.7
Determining the Coordinates

■ Firstly, use **FORMAT/Units** to ensure that the coordinate unit precision is set to **2** decimal places in the **Drawing Units** dialogue box as shown in Figure 7.4.

■ Use **TOOLS/Inquiry/ ID Point** to ascertain the coordinates of the **Centre** of the largest circle to obtain the coordinates and enter in the box as required (Answer - 135.18, 157.36).

Figure 7.4 The Units Control dialogue box with the units precision set to two decimal places

3.8

Fitting the Curve

■ To fit the curve as required use **MODIFY/Polyline** and **Fit** a curve to the lower polyline.

■ Use **MODIFY/Extend** to lengthen the vertical line to meet the curved line.

3.9

Editing the House Drawing

■ Type the variable **MIRRTEXT** at the command line and set to **0** to prevent the text being reversed when we use **MODIFY/Mirror** to copy the house, using the **END**points of the vertical line as the first and second mirror points as shown in Figure 7.5.

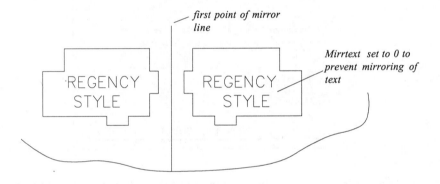

Figure 7.5 *The completed house drawing with mirroring and text non-reversed*

3.10

Entering Your Details

■ Enter your name and the date in the box provided using **DRAW/Text/Single Line Text**.

3.11

Saving the Drawing

■ To save the drawing use **FILE/Save As** and save the completed project to your floppy disk or to a folder with the name PA7AE.

If you use **FILE/Save** AutoCAD will perform a quick save and overwrite the original unedited drawing.

Target Drawing - PA7A - Part Two

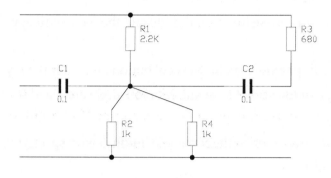

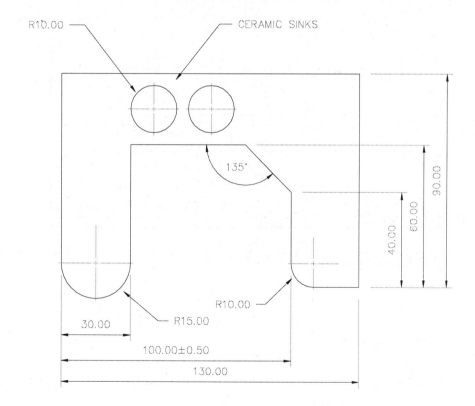

3.12

Inserting the Drawing PA7B

- Activate AutoCAD to open drawing **PA7C**.

- Your tutor will provide you with the location of the pre-prepared drawing **PA7B** which you are required to place in the drawing at coordinates **5, 245**.

- Use **INSERT/Block** and click on **Browse** to locate the file and the name will appear as shown in Figure 7.6.

- Remove the check in the '**Specify parameters on Screen**' button and enter the x,y coordinates of **5, 245** ensuring that the scale factor and rotation angle are **1** and **0** respectively.

  (You can also specify the coordinate position on the command line instead of specifying them here if you don't remove the check).

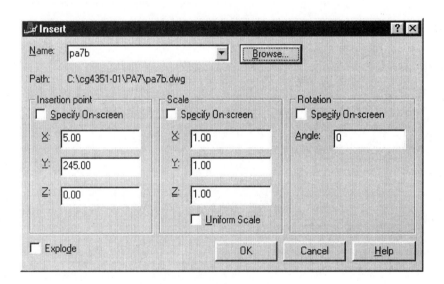

Figure 7.6 *The Insert dialogue box*

3.13
Creating a User Coordinate System

The Model Space UCS icon can be repositioned in the drawing to create a user-coordinate system with an origin specified by the user. This position then becomes the origin of the drawing.
We are required to move the origin of the drawing to the end of the lower left hand line of drawing **PA7B**.

■ Use **TOOLS/Move UCS** and specify the new origin at the **Endpoint** of the line as required. At this stage the icon may not physically move to the end of the line.

■ Use **VIEW/Display/UCS Icon/Origin** to display the icon at its new position.

■ To save the new UCS position with the name **CIRCUIT**, type **UCS** at the command line and **Save** the name.

■ To ensure that the UCS icon is visible at this position use **VIEW/Display/UCS Icon/On**.

3.14/3.15
Creating the Blocks and Producing the Electronic Diagram

This part of the exercise requires us to create two blocks with attribute data attached. The mode of the attribute data varies, enabling the user to alter the data contents of the block at insertion time and with prompts appearing, originated by the user.
The method is to draw the outline of the required drawing, create the attribute data for each incidence of an attribute (in this case we will have to define a variable attribute three times each for the blocks **'CAP'** and **'RES'**) and lastly, save the drawing and attribute data as a block.

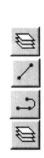

■ Make the **Current** layer **Outline**.

■ Use **DRAW/Line** and **Polyline** to draw the outline of the shape **'CAP'** in any area of the PA7C drawing.

■ Make the **Current** layer **Number**.

■ Use **DRAW/Block/Define Attributes** and the **Attribute Definition** dialogue box appears as shown in Figure 7.7.

■ Type in the tag **'T1'**, the prompt **'ENTER NUMBER'** (i.e. every time the block is inserted into the drawing, the user will be prompted to enter data for the electronic block (in this case **C1** or **C2**) and the default value **'C1'**.

■ Enter the required text style and height.

■ Use **Pick Point** to choose the position for the tag above the boundary of the **'CAP'** drawing as shown in Figure 7.7.

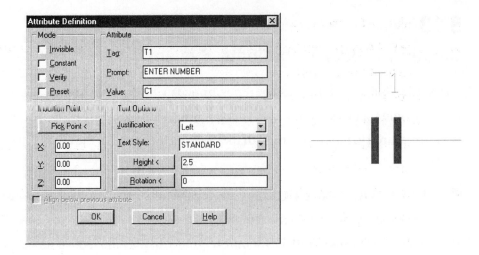

Figure 7.7 The Attribute Definition dialogue box and the Cap drawing with first variable attribute

- Make the **Current** layer **Value**.

- Use **DRAW/Block/Define Attributes** again to create the second attribute. The **Attribute Definition** dialogue box appears as shown in Figure 7.8 and again the attribute mode is variable. You will see from the dialogue box in Figure 7.8 that as the attribute can vary in its value, a meaningful prompt to the user needs to be included.

- Use **Pick Point** to choose the position underneath the **CAP** drawing as shown in Figure 7.8.

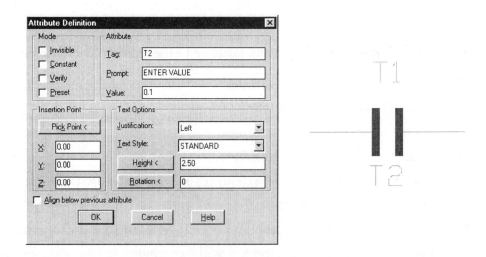

Figure 7.8 The Attribute Definition dialogue box with the second variable attribute positioned

■ Make the **Current** layer **Cost**.

■ Use **DRAW/Block/Define Attributes** once more to create the third attribute. The **Attribute Definition** dialogue box appears as shown in Figure 7.9 and again the attribute mode is variable but this time it is invisible i.e. it does not automatically appear in the block as data unless prompted with the **ATTDISP/ON** command. You will see again from the dialogue box in Figure 7.9 that as the attribute can vary in its value, a meaningful prompt to the user needs to be included.

■ Click on the '**Align below previous attribute button**' and the tag is placed as shown in Figure 7.9. (the instructions state to position the attribute next to the previous two, but when inserted in the drawing, it interferes with the connecting lines).

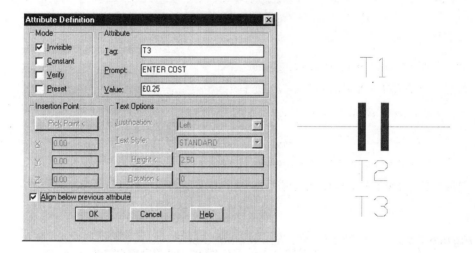

Figure 7.9 *The Attribute Definition dialogue box with the third variable attribute positioned*

Creating a Block of the Drawing

- Make the **Current** layer **Outline**.
- To create a block of the **CAP** drawing to include its attributes, use **DRAW/Block/Make** and the **Block Definition** dialogue box will appear as shown in Figure 7.10.
- Enter the name, and click on **Select point** to choose the **Endpoint** of the line as its insertion base point as required.
- Lastly, **Select Objects** and select the outline and attribute tags. The block will stay on screen as separate objects if **Retain Objects** is checked.

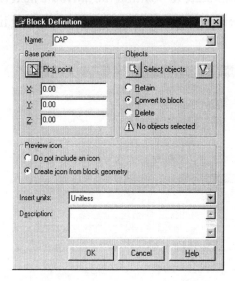

Figure 7.10   *The Block Definition dialogue box*

- Make the **Current** layer **Outline**.
- Use **DRAW/Line** to draw the outline of the shape **'RES'** in any area of the PA7C drawing.
- Repeat the sequence exactly as you did for the making of the **'CAP'** block including the layer changes.

3.16
Creating the Blocks as Separate Drawings

Creating a block in a drawing makes that block available to that drawing only. To be able to insert the block in any other drawing we can create the block as a separate drawing using the **WBLOCK** command (which stands for 'Write Block').

- Type **WBLOCK** at the command line and the **Write Block** dialogue box will appear as shown in Figure 7.11.

- Click on **Block** as the **Source** and scroll through the pull-down list and choose the **CAP** block.

- Enter the file name **CAP** under **Destination/Filename** and choose the file location in this portion also.

- Click on **OK**.

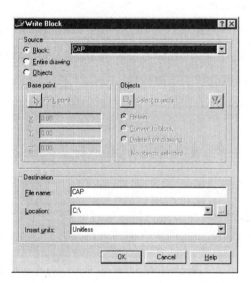

Figure 7.11   *The Write Block dialogue box*

- Repeat the operation for the **'RES'** Wblock.

3.17
Completing the Electronic Diagram

- Firstly, make layer **0** the **Current** layer.
- Use **DRAW/Line** to draw the line from coordinates **48, 40 Perpendicular** to the middle line as shown in Figure 7.12.
- Repeat the operation for the line starting at **118, 40** as shown in Figure 7.12.
- Use **INSERT/Block** to insert the **CAP** blocks onto the **Endpoints** of the middle lines adding the correct attribute values as required.
- The 'invisible' Cost attribute remains as the default value.
- Repeat **INSERT/Block** for the **RES** block numbers **R1**, **R3** and **R4,** again adding the correct attribute values as required.
- To insert the **RES** block **R2**, firstly use **TOOLS/Inquiry/ID Point** to identify the coordinate value of the left hand **Endpoint** of the bottom line. This is done merely to enable us to specify an insertion point relative to it.
- Use **INSERT/Block** and when asked for the **Insertion point** type **@39.333, 0** or **39.3333<0,** whichever you prefer. (39.3333 is one third of 118).
- Complete the required attributes as before.

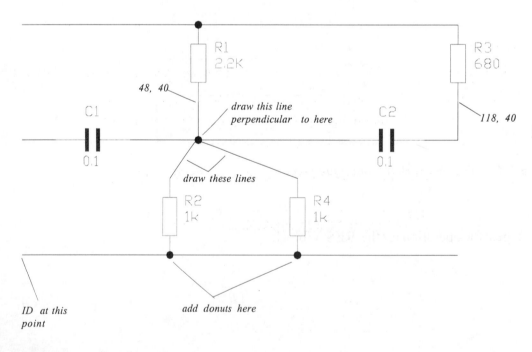

Figure 7.12 *The Electrical diagram*

3.18

Adding Lines and Filled Circles

- Use **DRAW/Line** to draw the lines to the **RES** blocks **R2** and **R4**.
- Use **DRAW/Donut** to place the donuts at the **Intersections** as shown in Figure 7.12.

3.19

Creating a Dimension Style

In preparation for dimensioning we are required to create an associative (grouped objects) dimension style called **CGTEST** on its own layer. This is done through the **DIMENSION/Style** command where the style attributes are applied and saved.

You may find it more convenient to complete the dimensions in the order as shown in figure 7.17.

- Use **FORMAT/DimensionStyle** to activate the **Dimension Style Manager** dialogue box.
- Click on the **New** button and the **Create New Dimension Style** dialogue box will overlay the first.
- Type in the name **CGTEST** and click the **Continue** button as shown in Figure 7.12.
- The **New Dimension Style** dialogue box will appear with the **Lines and Arrows** tab active.
- Change the values to those described in objective 3.21. Some are highlighted with a black rectangle as shown in Figure 7.13.
- Repeat the operation for **Text** and **Tolerances** as shown in Figures 7.14 and 7.15 respectively.
- In the **Primary Units** tab dialogue box click on **Precision** and change the values so that the linear precision is to 2 decimal places as shown in Figure 7.16.
- Click on **OK** and the **Dimension Style Manager** dialogue box reappears.
- Click on the style name **CGTEST**, **Set Current** and **Close**.

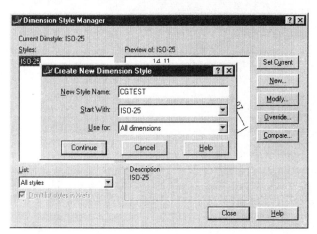

Figure 7.12 *The Dimension Style Manager dialogue box with the CGTEST style created*

changes colour of dimension lines

changes spacing of baseline dimensions

changes colour of extension lines

changes distance of extension line

changes distance of extension line from chosen object

changes size of arrowhead

changes size of centre mark

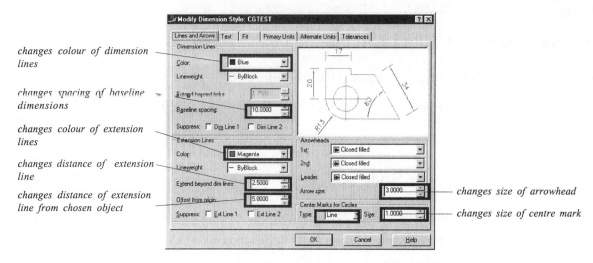

Figure 7.13   *The Lines and Arrows tab dialogue box with the required changes highlighted*

sets the text font

sets the text colour

sets the text height

Positions text centred above dimension line

Places text in relation to the dimension line

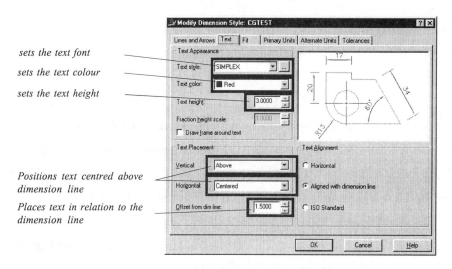

Figure 7.14   *The Text tab dialogue box with the required changes highlighted*

sets the tolerance method

sets the tolerance precision

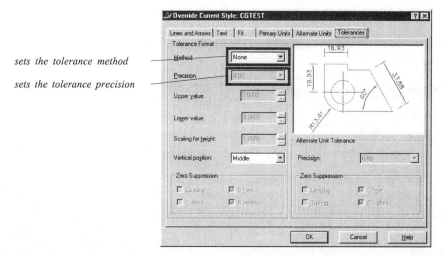

Figure 7.15   *The Tolerances tab dialogue box with the required changes highlighted*

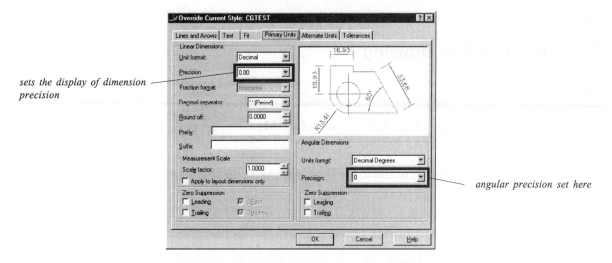

sets the display of dimension precision

angular precision set here

Figure 7.16 *The Primary Units tab dialogue box with changes highlighted*

You can now dimension the drawing by following the instructions in objective 3.21.

3.20

Creating a New Layer

- Activate the **Layer** dialogue box by using **FORMAT/Layer**.
- Click on **New** and the word **Layer1** will appear in the list.
- Simply overtype this with **CGDIMENS**.

3.21
Dimensioning the Drawing

a)

- Use **FORMAT/Layer** to make the layer **CGDIMENS Current**.
- Click on **OK**.

- Use **DIMENSIONS/Style** and in the **Dimensions Style** dialogue box ensure that **CGTEST** is **Set Current**.

b)

To ensure that all dimensions are associative, the system variable **DIMASO**, which defaults to **On**, needs to remain in that state.
- Type **DIMASO** at the command line and ensure that it is **On**.

c)

To prevent dimensions overlapping the Dimension line spacing needs to be set to a suitable figure. We have set our spacing to **10** as shown in the **Text** tab dialogue box, Figure 7.13.

d)

- To ensure that a degree symbol is inserted in the dimension line we need to use the **Primary Units** tab dialogue box as shown in Figure 7.16 with **Angular Dimension Precision** which is set to **0**.

e)

- The plus/minus tolerance limits are set through the **Tolerances** tab dialogue box as shown in Figure 7.15 with the **Tolerance Format Method** set to **Deviation**.

f)

- The text for radius dimensions is completed with the **DIMENSION/Leader** command and the text format in the middle of the line is set through the **Text** tab dialogue box as shown in Figure 7.14.

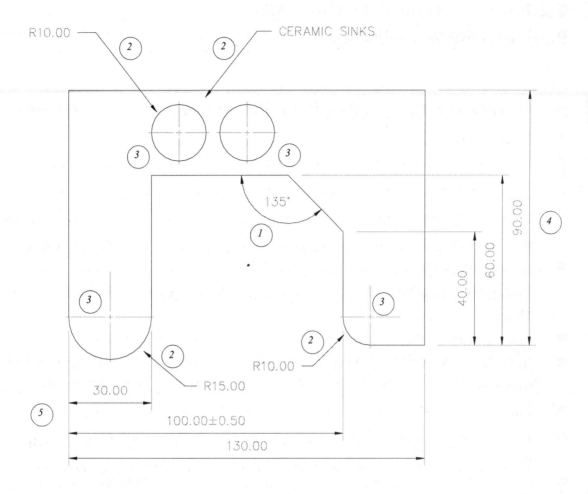

Figure 7.17 The completed PA7CE drawing

1

- In the **Dimension Style Manager** dialogue box click on **Override**.
- To enter the angular value, in the **DIMENSION/Style Text** tab dialogue box change the **Vertical Text Placement** to **JIS**.
- Put a check mark in the **Inside Horizontal Text** box.
- In the **Text Placement** change the **Offset from dim Line** to **3**.
- In the **Primary Units** tab dialogue box set the **Angular Dimension Precision** to **0**.
- **OK** through the dialogue boxes but do not save the changes.
- Use **DIMENSION/Angular** and place the angle as required.

2

- In the **Dimension Style Manager** dialogue box click on **Override**.
- To enter the leader values, in the **DIMENSION/Style Text** tab dialogue box change the **Vertical Text Placement** to **Centred**.

- Draw the leader and text **'CERAMIC SINKS'**.
- Repeat the operation for the three other leaders and enter the radius text.

3

- To place the Centre Marks use **DIMENSION/Center Marks** and select the arcs and circles.

4

- The 'stacked' dimensions at the bottom and left of the drawing are achieved through setting the **Dimension Lines Baseline Spacing** in the **Lines and Arrows** tab dialogue box, which we have already set, to a value of **10**.
- In addition, the distance between the extension line and the endpoint of the measured object is set through the **Text** tab dialogue box with the **Extension Line Offset from Origin** as shown in Figure 7.17.

- In the **Dimension Style Manager** dialogue box click on **Override**.
- In the **DIMENSION/Style Text** tab dialogue box change the **Vertical Text Placement** to **Above**.
- Put a check mark in the **Aligned with Dimension line** box.
- In the **Primary Units** tab dialogue box set the **Angular Dimension Precision** to **2** decimal places.

- To draw the distance of **40.00** at the right of the drawing use **DIMENSION/Linear** and choose the bottom right hand **ENDpoint** of the line and the **Intersection** of the start of the angled line.
- Use **DIMENSION/Baseline** and select the second dimension line origin at the end of the angled line to insert the **60.00** dimension.
- Repeat the **Baseline** command for the **90.00** dimension.

5

- Use **DIMENSION/Linear**, select the **Endpoint** of the semicircle arc and place the text of **30.00** units.
- In the **Dimension Style Manager** dialogue box click on **Override**.
- In the **Tolerances** tab dialogue box set the **ToleranceFormat Method** to **Symmetrical**, and an **Upper Value** of **0.5**.
- Ensure that the **Units Tolerance Precision** is set to **2** decimal places as shown in Figure 7.15.
- **OK** and **Close** through the dialogue boxes.

■ Using **DIMENSION/Baseline**, select the endpoint of the second extension (the **Endpoint** of the arc) and the dimension will be placed **10** units under the previous.

 ■ In the **Dimension Style Manager** dialogue box click on **Override**.

■ In the **Tolerances** tab dialogue box set the **ToleranceFormat Method** to **None**.

■ Complete the remaining baseline dimension of **130.00**.

■ (An alternative to this, which I prefer, is to complete these three baseline dimensions but without setting the **Tolerance Format Method** to **Symmetrical**.

■ After completing them, change the **Tolerance Format Method** to **Symmetrical** with the **Upper Value of 0.5**.

■ **OK** and **Close** through the boxes.

■ Use **DIMENSION/Update** and click on the **100.00** dimension and it will be updated to the required style.)

3.22
Saving the View

 ■ To save the view of the titlebox use **VIEW/Zoom/Window** and place a zoom window around the box ensuring that only the box is visible on screen.

■ At the command line type **VIEW** and the **View** dialogue box will appear.

■ Click on **New** and the **New View** dialogue box will overlay the previous.

■ Type **Title** as the **View Name**.

■ Click on **OK** in both dialogue boxes**.**

3.23
Editing the Titlebox Attributes

We are required to edit the attributes in the titlebox to provide your own name and date.

 ■ Use **MODIFY/Attribute/Single** and overwrite the current details with your own as shown in Figure 7.18.

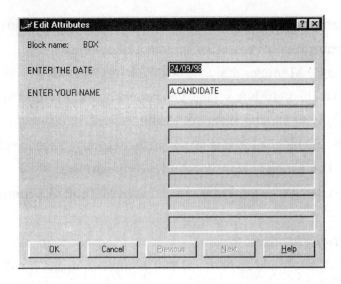

Figure 7.18 *The Edit Attributes dialogue box*

3.24

Changing the Text Style Name and Removing Unused layers

To change the name of the text style called **Title** to **Title2**

- Use **FORMAT/Rename** and the **Rename** dialogue box appears as shown in Figure 7.19.
- Select **Text styles** and then the **Item** called **Title**.
- Enter **Title2** in the **Rename** box .
- Click on **OK**.

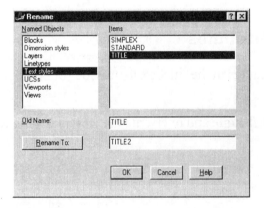

Figure 7.19 *The Rename dialogue box*

- To remove the unused linetype pattern **Phantom** from the drawing we can use **FILE/ Drawing Utilities/Purge/Linetype** and the command line will prompt

Command: _purge
Enter type of unused objects to purge
[Blocks/Dimstyles/LAyers/LTypes/Plotstyles/SHapes/textSTyles/Mlinestyles/All] :
_lt Enter name(s) to purge <>:*   **Phantom**
Verify each name to be purged? [Yes/No] <Y>:   **Enter**
Purge linetype PHANTOM? <N>   *y*

3.25

Saving the Drawing

- To save the drawing use **FILE/Save As** and save the completed project to your selected folder or directory.

If you use **File/Save** AutoCAD will perform a quick save to the original PA7C drawing.

3.26

Copying the Completed Drawing Files

- To copy the drawing files from your folder, right click on the **Start** button and click on **Explore**.
- Locate the folder and files.
- Click on the files, either singly, or with the **CTRL** key held down, select them simultaneously and drag the files to the floppy drive icon.

Target Drawing - Part 1 - PA8A

DRAWING 1

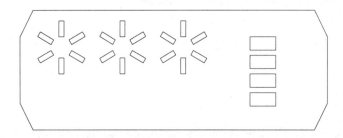

DRAWING 2

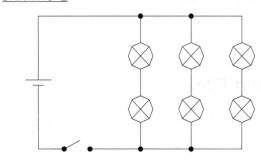

CITY & GUILDS	
NAME	
DATE	
COORDINATES	

DRAWING 3

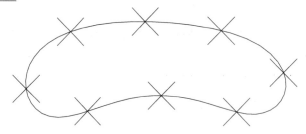

Pre-prepared files

To complete this assignment the pre-prepared drawings **PA8A**, **PA8B** and **PA8C** are needed.

Your tutor will provide you with the location of these files.

You may also download the files from the publisher's website at www.payne-gallway.co.uk.

3.2

Copying the Drawing Files

- To copy the drawing files from the floppy disk, right click on the **Start** button and click on **Explore**.

- Click the floppy drive icon and click on the files, either singly, or with the **CTRL** key held down select them simultaneously and drag the files to the folder.

- Execute AutoCAD and **Open** the drawing **PA8A**.

3.3

Editing the Sheet Metal Component

To produce the completed sheet metal component we need to array the slots and chamfer the corners.

- To locate the centre of the array in relation to the top left hand corner use **TOOLS/Inquiry/ ID point** and select the corner as shown in Figure 8.1. We can now place a point marker at the centre of the array with coordinates relative to that corner.

- Use **DRAW/Point**

  Command: _point Point: @16, -14   (relative coordinates)
  Command:

- Use **MODIFY/Array/Polar** to copy the slot with **6** items for **360°**, rotating as they are copied. The base point is the **Node** of the point as shown in Figure 8.1.

- Use **MODIFY/Array/Rectangular** to copy the **6** slots with **1 row**, **3 columns** and **24** between the columns.

- For the rectangular slot use **MODIFY/Array/Rectangular** again, with **4** rows, **1** column and **-7** between the rows (don't forget the minus).

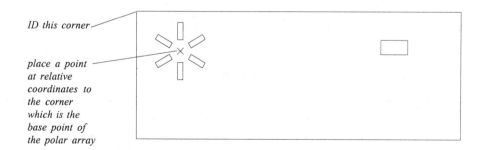

Figure 8.1 *The Sheet Metal Component showing the arrayed objects*

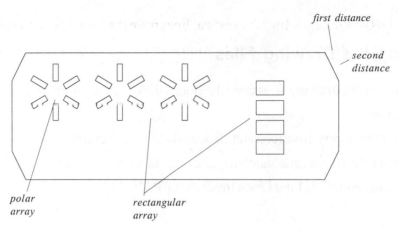

first distance

second distance

polar array

rectangular array

Figure 8.2 *The completed Sheet Metal Plate showing the arrayed objects*

- Use **MODIFY/Chamfer** to angle the metal plate corners with a first distance of **5** and second distance of **10** as shown in Figure 8.2.

- Use **MODIFY/Erase** to delete the point.

3.4
Editing the Block Object

The original drawing is created as a block and, as it needs to be re-sized it will need to be broken down to its individual objects. It can then be stretched and the extra components added. The moving of the original parts can be achieved quickly with the Stretch command (remember to pick the objects with a crossing window).

- Firstly, **MODIFY/Explode** the block into its individual objects.
- Use **MODIFY/ Stretch** to resize the entity upwards with a crossing window as shown in Figure 8.3, using the base point and with **@10<90** (or **@0,10**).
- **MODIFY/Stretch** the two horizontal lines and the vertical left hand line picking the **Intersection** as the base point as shown in Figure 8.3 and the second point of displacement **@5<90**. This will move the small horizontal lines up by 5 units.
- **MODIFY/Stretch** the two circles with the enclosed crosses and two vertical lines joining them, using the base point of one of the circle **Centre**s and a second point of displacement **@15<90**. This will move the circles up by 15 units.
- **MODIFY/Copy** the two circles and their internal crosses picking the **Centre** of a circle as the base point and a second point **@20<270** for the first set downwards.
- Repeat the **MODIFY/Copy** command to copy the two inner circles to the left by **20** units.

■ Use **DRAW/Line** to draw the vertical lines from the circle **Quadrants** (12 and 6 o'clock positions) **PERPendicular** to the upper and lower horizontal lines as shown in Figure 8.4.

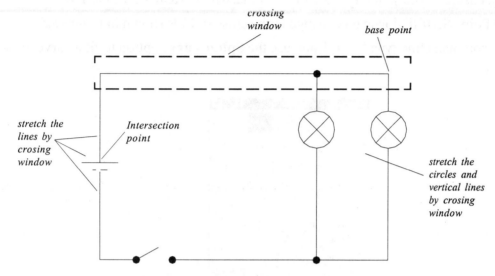

Figure 8.3 *The stretched components of the exploded block*

■ Use **DRAW/Donut** with zero inner radius and **2** outer radius and place at the **INTersections** of the vertical and horizontal lines.

■ Lastly, you will need to move the words **'Drawing 2'** upwards.

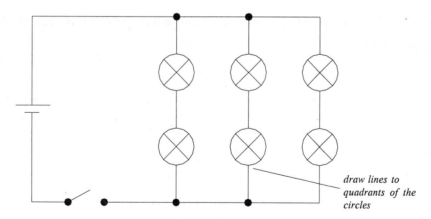

Figure 8.4 *The completed component with new lines drawn to the quadrants of the circles*

3.5
Fitting a Spline Curve

- Firstly, ensure that the point style is in the 'x' format with **FORMAT/Point Style**.
- In the **Point Style** dialogue box change to the cross style as shown in Figure 8.5.
- At the command line type **PEDIT** and use the **Spline curve** option to fit a curve to the polyline.

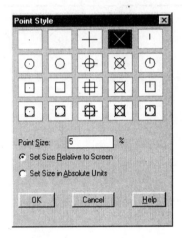

Figure 8.5 *The Points Style dialogue box*

3.6
Scaling the Object

- Use **MODIFY/Scale** to resize the polyline using a base point of co-ords **50, 40** and to **1.25** of its original size.

3.7

Editing the Outline

- Use **MODIFY/Point/Divide** to mark the polyline into **8** segments.
- Ensure that the **Units Length Precision** is to **2** decimal places with the **FORMAT/Units** dialogue box.
- Use **TOOLS/Inquiry/ID Point** at the **Node** of the required point to find the X, Y coordinates as shown in Figure 8.5 (Answer: 131.50, 76.59).

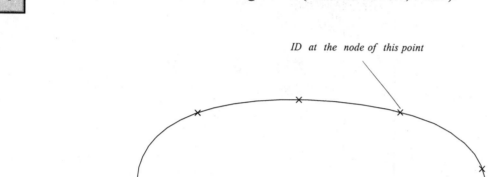

ID at the node of this point

Figure 8.5 *The polyline with points placed around the circle*

3.8

Entering Your Details

- Enter your name and the date in the box provided using **DRAW/Text/Single Line Text**.

3.9

Saving the Drawing

- To save the drawing use **FILE/Save As** and save the completed project to your floppy disk or to a folder with the name PA8AE.

If you use **FILE/Save** AutoCAD will perform a quick save and overwrite the original unedited drawing.

4351-01- PA8
Target Drawing - PA8B - Part Two

MACHINING CENTRE

3 AXIS

MACHINING CENTRE

5 AXIS

TURNING CENTRE

CNC SLANT BED

TURNING CENTRE

CNC SLANT BED

CITY. & GUILDS
NAME A.CANDIDATE
DATE 24/09/98

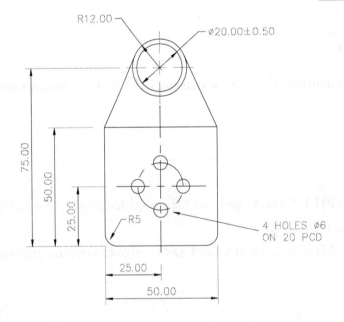

R12.00

Ø20.00±0.50

75.00

50.00

25.00

R5

4 HOLES ø6
ON 20 PCD

25.00

50.00

3.10

Inserting the Drawing PA8B

- Activate AutoCAD to open drawing **PA8C**. Your tutor will provide you with the location of the pre-prepared drawing **PA8B** which you are required to place in the drawing at coordinates **15, 170**.

- Use **INSERT/Block** and click on **Browse** to locate the file **PA8B**.

- Check off the **'Specify parameters on Screen'** button and enter the x,y coordinates of **15, 170** ensuring that the scale factor and rotation angle are **1** and **0** respectively. (You can also specify the coordinate position on the command line instead of specifying them here).

3.11

Creating a User Coordinate System

The Model Space UCS icon can be repositioned in the drawing to create a user-coordinate system with an origin specified by the user. This position then becomes the origin of the drawing. We are required to move the origin of the drawing to the end of the left hand line of drawing **PA8B**.

- Use **TOOLS/Move UCS** and pick the **Endpoint** of the line as required. At this stage the icon may not physically move to the end of the line.

- Use **VIEW/Display/UCS Icon/Origin** to display the icon at its new position.

- To save the new UCS position with the name **FACTORY**, type **UCS** at the command line and **Save**.

- To ensure that the UCS icon is visible at this position use **VIEW/Display/UCS Icon/On**.

3.12/3.13
Creating the Blocks and Producing the Machine Tool Layout

This part of the exercise requires us to create two blocks with attribute data attached. The mode of the attribute data varies, enabling the user to alter the data contents of the block at insertion time and with prompts appearing, originated by the user.

The method is to draw the outline of the required drawing, create the attribute data for each incidence of an attribute (in this case we will have to define one constant attribute and two variable attributes each for the blocks 'MC' and 'TC') and lastly, save the drawing and attribute data as a block.

- Make the **Current** layer **Outline**.
- Turn **Grid** and **Snap** on with values of **5**.
- Use **DRAW/Line** (or polyline) to draw the outline of the shape 'MC' in any area of the PA8C drawing, snapping to the grid intersections to quickly draw the shape.
- Use **MODIFY/Fillet** to fillet the radius of the square with a **5** unit radius.
- Make the **Current** layer **Name**.
- Use **DRAW/Block/Define Attributes** and the **Attribute Definition** dialogue box appears as shown in Figure 8.6.
- Type in the tag 'T1'.
- Type in the value 'MACHINING CENTRE'.
- Place a check in the **Constant** box to make the attribute non-changeable.
- Enter the required text style and height.
- Use **Pick Point** to choose the position for the tag above the boundary of the 'MC' drawing as shown in Figure 8.6.

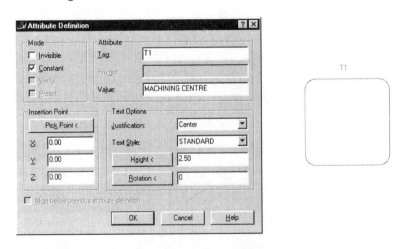

Figure 8.6 *The Attribute Definition dialogue box and the MC drawing with first constant attribute*

- Make the **Current** layer **Type**.
- Use **DRAW/Block/Define Attributes** again to create the second attribute. The **Attribute Definition** dialogue box appears as shown in Figure 8.7 and this time the attribute mode is variable. You will see from the dialogue box in Figure 8.7 that as the attribute can vary in its value, a meaningful **Prompt** to the user needs to be included.
- Use **Pick Point** to choose the position in the middle of the **MC** drawing as shown in Figure 8.7.

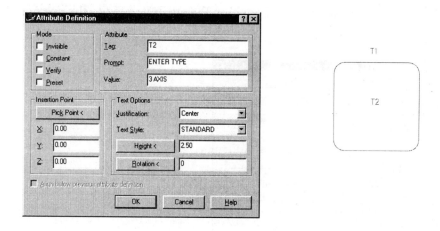

Figure 8.7   *The Attribute Definition dialogue box and the MC drawing with second variable attribute*

- Make the **Current** layer **Cost**.
- Use **DRAW/Block/Define Attributes** once more to create the third attribute. The **Attribute Definition** dialogue box appears as shown in Figure 8.8 and again the attribute mode is variable but this time it is invisible i.e. it does not automatically appear in the block as data unless prompted with the **ATTDISP/On** command. You will see again from the dialogue box in Figure 8.8 that as the attribute can var in its value, a meaningful prompt to the user needs to be included.
- Click on the '**Align below previous attribute button**' and the tag is placed as shown in Figure 8.8 (the instructions state to position the attribute next to the previous two, but I have placed it below the previous).

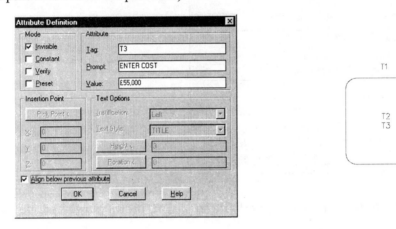

Figure 8.8 *The Attribute Definition dialogue box and the MC drawing with third variable/hidden attribute*

- Repeat the operation for the **TC** block including the layer changes.

- Make the **Current** layer **Outline**.

- To create a block of the drawing to include its attributes, use **DRAW/Block/Make** and the **Block Definition** dialogue box will appear as shown in Figure 8.9.

- Enter the name, and choose the **gridpoint** (turn **Snap On**) just off the bottom left corner of the line as its insertion base point as required.

- Lastly, **Select Objects** and select the outline and attribute tags. The block will stay on screen as separate objects if **Retain Objects** is checked.

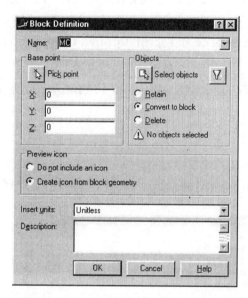

Figure 8.9 The Block Definition dialogue box

- Ensure that the **Current** layer is **Outline**.
- Ensure that **Grid** and **Snap** are **On** and a value of **5**.
- Repeat the sequence as you did for the **MC** block including the layer changes and create the **TC** block.

3.14
Creating the Blocks as Separate Drawings

Creating a block in a drawing makes that block available to that drawing only. To be able to insert the block in any other drawing we can create the block as a separate drawing using the **WBLOCK** command (which stands for 'Write Block').

- Type **WBLOCK** at the command line and the **Write Block** dialogue box will appear as shown in Figure 8.10.
- Click on **Block** as the **Source** and scroll through the pull-down list and choose the **MC** block.
- Enter the file name **MC** under **Destination/ Filename** and choose the file location in this portion also.
- Click on **OK**.

The MC block has now been created as a separate drawing called **MC.dwg**.

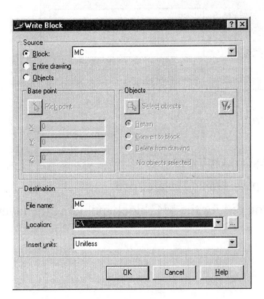

Figure 8.10 The Write Block dialogue box

- Repeat the operation of creating the Wblock for the **'TC'** drawing.

3.15

Completing the Machine Tool Layout

- To insert the **3axis MC** block use **INSERT/Block** and the **Insert** dialogue box will appear.

- Click on the **Name** pull-down, and click on **MC** .

- Click on **OK**.

- The Command line prompts for an insertion point (if the **Specify on Screen** box is checked enter the coordinates **14, 75**).

- Accept the attribute default values.

- Repeat the process for coordinates **4, 10** changing the **Type** to **5 Axis**.

- To insert the **TC** block at $^1/_3$ and $^1/_4$ from the bottom intersection, firstly we can use **TOOLS/Inquiry/ID Point** to ascertain the coordinates at that corner as shown in Figure 8.11 and then **Insert** the TC block by specifying relative coordinates to that point .

Command: ***id***   (***pick** the Intersection as shown in Figure 8.11)*
Specify point: _int of X = 87   Y = 0   Z = 0

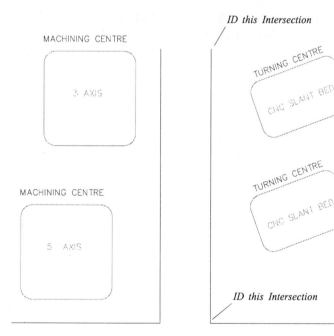

Figure 8.11 *The ID point for locating the TC blocks relatively*

- Use **INSERT/Block** and the **Insert** dialogue box will appear.
- Scroll through the **Name** pull-down and click on **TC**.
- Enter **20** in the **Angle Rotation**.
- Ensure that the **Insertion Point -Specify On screen** box is checked.
- Click on **OK**.
- Accept the attribute default values.

Command: ***_insert***
Specify insertion point or [Scale/X/Y/Z/Rotate/PScale/PX/PY/PZ/PRotate]: ***@24.666, 29*** *($^1/_3$ of 74 and $^1/_4$ of 116)*

Enter X scale factor, specify opposite corner, or [Corner/XYZ] <1>:   ***Enter***
Enter Y scale factor <use X scale factor>:   ***Enter***

- To insert the second **TC** block use **TOOLS/Inquiry/ID Point** and pick the top of the right hand vertical line as shown in Figure 8.11.
- We can now place the block with relative coordinates once again.

- Use **INSERT/Block** and the **Insert** dialogue box will appear again.
- Enter **20** in the **Angle Rotation**.
- Click on **OK**.
- Change the attribute default values to those required.

Command: ***_ddinsert***
Insertion point: ***@24.666,-38.666*** *(don't forget the minus) ($^1/_3$ of 74 and $^1/_3$ of 116)*
X scale factor <1> / Corner / XYZ: ***Enter***
Y scale factor (default=X):   ***Enter***

3.16

Creating a Dimension Style

In preparation for dimensioning we are required to create an associative (grouped objects) dimension style called **CGTEST** on its own layer. This is done through the **DIMENSION/ Style** command where the style attributes are applied and saved.

You may find it more convenient to complete the dimensions in the order as shown in figure 8.16.

- Use **FORMAT/DimensionStyle** to activate the **Dimension Style Manager** dialogue box.
- Click on the **New** button and the **Create New Dimension Style** dialogue box will overlay the first.
- Type in the name **CGTEST** and click the **Continue** button as shown in Figure 8.12.

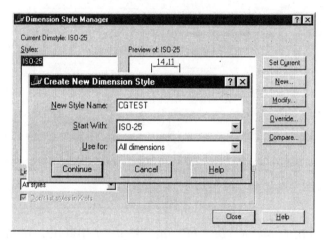

Figure 8.12   *The Dimension Style Manager dialogue box with the CGTEST style created*

- The **Dimension Style Manager** dialogue box will appear with the **Lines and Arrows** tab active.
- Change the values to those described in objective 3.18. Some are highlighted with a black rectangle as shown in Figure 8.13.
- Repeat the operation for **Text** and **Tolerances** as shown in Figures 8.14 and 8.15 respectively.
- In the **Primary Units** tab dialogue box click on **Precision** and change the values so that the linear precision is to **2** places as shown in Figure 8.16.
- Click on **OK** and the **Dimension Style Manager** dialogue box reappears.
- Click on the style name **CGTEST**, **Set Current** and **Close**.

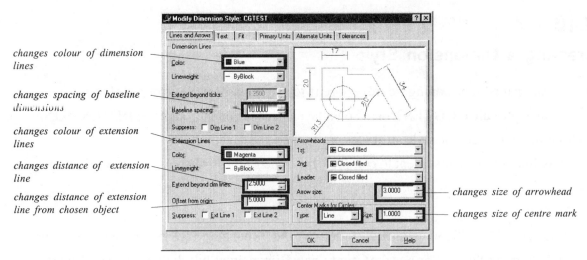

changes colour of dimension
lines

changes spacing of baseline
dimensions

changes colour of extension
lines

changes distance of extension
line

changes distance of extension
line from chosen object

changes size of arrowhead

changes size of centre mark

Figure 8.13 *The Lines and Arrows tab dialogue box with the required changes highlighted*

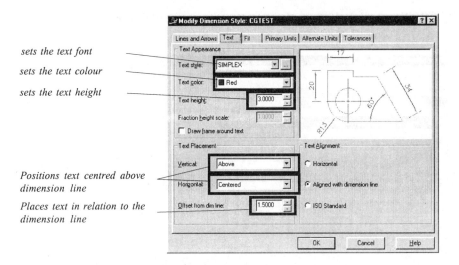

sets the text font

sets the text colour

sets the text height

Positions text centred above
dimension line

Places text in relation to the
dimension line

Figure 8.14 *The Text tab dialogue box with the required changes highlighted*

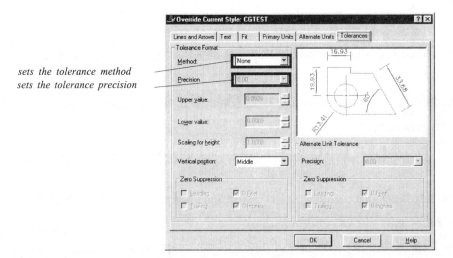

sets the tolerance method
sets the tolerance precision

Figure 8.15 *The Tolerances tab dialogue box with the required changes highlighted*

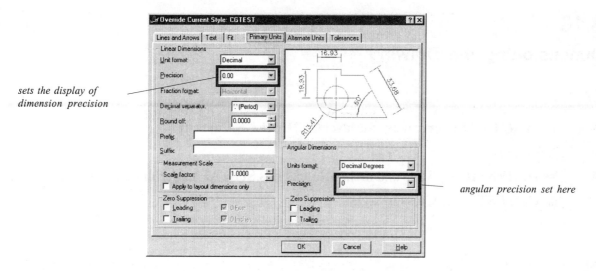

sets the display of dimension precision

angular precision set here

Figure 8.16 *The Primary Units tab dialogue box with changes highlighted*

You can now dimension the drawing by following the instructions in objective 3.18.

3.17

Creating a New Layer

■ Activate the **Layer** dialogue box by using **FORMAT/Layer**.

■ Click on **New** and the word **Layer1** will appear in the list. Simply overtype this with **CGDIMENS**.

3.18

Dimensioning the Drawing

a)

- Use **FORMAT/Layer** to make the layer **CGDIMENS Current**.
- Click on **OK**.

- Use **DIMENSIONS/Style** and in the **Dimensions Style Manager** dialogue box ensure that **CGTEST** is the **Current** style.

b)

To ensure that all dimensions are associative, the system variable **DIMASO**, which defaults to **On**, needs to remain in that state.

- Type **DIMASO** at the command line and ensure that it is **On**.

c)

To prevent dimensions overlapping the Dimension line spacing needs to be set to a suitable figure. We have set our spacing to **10** as shown in the **Lines and Arrows** tab dialogue box, Figure 8.12.

d)

- To ensure that the Leader notes are inserted correctly we need to set the **Vertical Text Placement** to **Centred** as shown in Figure 8.13. It is initially set to **Above** to acommodate the other dimensions but will change as dimensioning progresses.

e)

- The plus/minus tolerance limits are set through the **Tolerance** tab dialogue box with the **Tolerance Format Method** set to **Deviation Precision** in the **Format** dialogue box and by changing the **Scaling for Height** value to **0.5**.

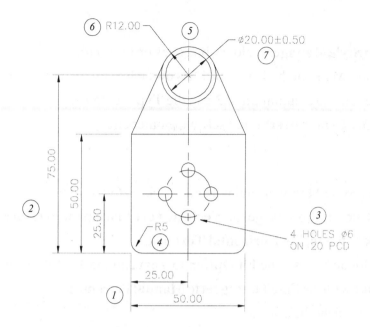

Figure 8.17 *The completed PA8CE drawing*

<u>*1/2*</u>

■ The 'stacked' dimensions at the bottom and left of the drawing are achieved through setting the **Baseline Spacing** in the **Lines and Arrows** tab dialogue box, which we have already set, to a value of **10**.

■ The distance between the extension line and the endpoint of the measured object is set through the same dialogue box with the **Offset from Origin** set to a suitable value.

■ To draw the vertical distance of **25.00** at the bottom of the drawing use **DIMENSION/ Linear** and choose the bottom left hand **END**point of the horizontal line and the **Endpoint** of the circle centre mark.

■ Use **DIMENSION/Baseline** and select the second dimension line origin at the **Endpoint** of the vertical line.

<u>*3/4*</u>

■ In the **Dimension Style Manager** dialogue box click on **Override**.

■ To enter the leader value, in the **Text** tab dialogue box change the **Vertical Text Placement** to **Centred**.

■ Put a check mark in the **Inside Horizontal Text** box.

■ Draw the leader, and text with text control code starting with '**4 HOLES %%C6**' and press **Enter**, completing the text on the next line.

■ Enter the text '**R5**'.

<u>5</u>

- In the **Dimension Style Manager** dialogue box click on **Override**.
- To place the Centre Mark, in the **Lines and Arrows** tab dialogue box set the **Centre Mark for Circles** size to a minimum of **3** and the **Type** set to **Line**.

- Use **DIMENSION/Center Marks** and select the outer circle.

<u>6</u>

- In the **Dimension Style Manager** dialogue box click on **Override**.
- In the **Text** tab dialogue box change the **Vertical Text Placement** to **Centred**.
- Put a check mark in the **Inside Horizontal Text** box.
- In the **Fit** tab dialogue box, set the **Fit Option** to **Text** and the **Text Placement** to **Beside the dimension line** with the **Fine Tuning** set to **Manual Placement**.
- **OK** and **Close** through the dialogue boxes.

- Using **DIMENSION/Radius**, select the inner circle and place the dimension.

<u>7</u>

- In the **Dimension Style Manager** dialogue box click on **Override**.
- In the **Tolerance** tab dialogue box set the **Tolerance Format Method** to **Symmetrical**, an **Upper Value** of **0.5** and a **Scaling for Height** of **1**.
- Ensure that the **Tolerance Format Precision** is set to two decimal places.
- In the **Fit** tab dialogue box, set the **Fit Option** to **Text** and the **Text Placement** to **Beside the dimension line** with the **Fine Tuning** set to **Manual Placement**.
- **OK** and **Close** through the dialogue boxes.
- Using **DIMENSION/Diameter**, select the inner circle and place the dimension.

3.19

Converting the Linetype

■ To change the dashed horizontal linetype to a **Continuous** style type **CHPROP** at the command line

Command:	*chprop*
Select objects: 1 found	***pick** the line*
Select objects:	***Enter***
Enter property to change [Color/LAyer/LType/ltScale/LWeight/Thickness]:	*lt (for linetype)*
Enter new linetype name <HIDDEN>:	***Continuous***
Enter property to change [Color/LAyer/LType/ltScale/LWeight/Thickness]:	***Enter***

3.20

Saving the View

■ To save the view of the titlebox use **VIEW/Zoom/Window** and place a zoom window around the box ensuring that only the box is visible on screen.

■ At the command line type **VIEW** and the **View** dialogue box will appear.

■ Click on **New** and the **New View** dialogue box will overlay the previous.

■ Type **Title** as the **View Name**.

■ Click on **OK** in both dialogue boxes.

3.21

Editing the Titlebox Attributes

We are required to edit the attributes in the titlebox to provide your own name and date.

 ■ Use **MODIFY/Attribute/Single** and overwrite the current details with your own as shown in Figure 8.18.

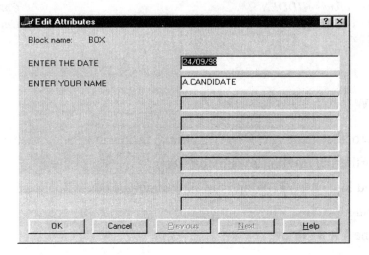

Figure 8.18 *The Edit Attributes dialogue box*

3.22

Changing the Linetype Name and Removing Unused Text Styles

- To change the name of the linetype called **Hidden** to **Special** use **FORMAT/Rename** and the **Rename** dialogue box appears as shown in Figure 8.18.

- Select **Linetype** and then select the **Item** called **Hidden**.

- Enter **Special** in the **Rename to** box.

- Click on **OK**.

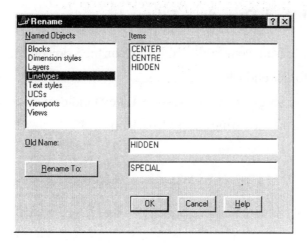

Figure 8.19 *The Rename Objects dialogue box*

- To remove the unused text style **Surplus** from the drawing we can use **FILE/Drawing Utilities/Purge/Text Styles** and the command line will prompt

```
Command: _purge
Enter type of unused objects to purge
[Blocks/Dimstyles/LAyers/LTypes/Plotstyles/SHapes/textSTyles/Mlinestyles/All]:
_st Enter name(s) to purge <*>:          surplus
Verify each name to be purged? [Yes/No] <Y>:      Enter
Purge text style "SURPLUS"? <N>                   y
```

3.23

Saving the Drawing

■ To save the drawing use **FILE/Save As** and save the completed project to your selected folder or directory.

If you use **File/Save** AutoCAD will perform a quick save to the original PA8C drawing.

3.24

Copying the Completed Drawing Files

■ To copy the drawing files from your folder, right click on the **Start** button and click on **Explore**. Locate the folder and files.

■ Click on the files, either singly, or with the **CTRL** key held down, select them simultaneously and drag the files to the floppy drive icon.

Congratulations!

You have completed the tuition part of the course. You will probably now need to repeat some of the exercises to become totally proficient. Follow that with some 'dry run' practising and you will be well prepared to sit the examinations.

Remember, of course that this book will not be made available to you during the examinations but, for the practical assignments, the AutoCAD manual should be.

If you have any constructive suggestions for improvements, questions or comments on the contents I'd be glad to hear from you.

You can contact me on my email address:- jeffroberts@72fernlea.freeserve.co.uk

Index

Ordering information

You can order by phone, fax, post or e-mail from our distributors:

BEBC Distribution
P.O. Box 3371
Poole
Dorset BH12 3YW

Tel: 01202 712909
Fax: 01202 712913
E-mail: pg@bebc.co.uk

Visit our web site at www.payne-gallway.co.uk for news about the latest titles and information about prices.

Also by Jeff Roberts:

Introduction to AutoCAD 2000

The book approaches the problem of learning AutoCAD from a new angle – a scenario is developed starting from a blank electronic drawing sheet and ending with a 3D drawing.
The final drawing shows 3 different views placed on a border with drawing titles etc.
It has been developed in this way to simulate, as closely as possible, how the drawing would be approached in a live situation. At the end of this book you should have gained the skills and confidence to attempt quite complex drawings.
The book can be used as an introduction to the City & Guilds 4351 series, The OCR Cambridge IT Certificate in CAD Module No. 115 and the BTEC Edexcel CAD project.

Teachers may order an inspection copy of the above book from BEBC.